Jesus - According To Thomas & Mary - and Me

Hello, Helen!

Watch out! Here is a slightly to greatly different view of Jesus! But enjoy as you can & share as you wish.

Gently,

Will Bessler
&
Nancy Shaw

742-7428

Jesus - According To Thomas & Mary - and Me

§

Francis William Bessler
2017

Featuring The Gospels of
THOMAS & MARY MAGDALENE
And
A Personal Interpretation
+
A Few Songs, concluding with:
The Same

Featuring
Mainly
The Gospels of
Thomas & Mary Magdalene
and
A Personal Interpretation

Copyright by
Francis William Bessler
Laramie, Wyoming
- 2017 –

ISBN: 1542618401
ISBN 13: 9781542618403

Introduction

§

HELLO! I AM SO VERY pleased to present the Gospels of the Apostles of Jesus named Thomas and Mary Magdalene in this work, combining two works I compiled in 2009 that I called JESUS VIA THOMAS COMMENTARIES and JESUS VIA MARY COMMENTARIES.

I will be presenting those two works directly; however I would like to comment on the name of this work: *JESUS ACCORDING TO THOMAS & MARY - AND ME* - because that name is important - especially the *AND ME* part of it.

As I will repeat in the included works of this compilation, I do believe that all "Scriptural" type verses are personal. That is to say that there is no such thing as an "objective" or "absolute" interpretation of any verse - be it so called "Scriptural" or otherwise. My interpretation is my own - just as any other person's interpretation of a same verse is his or her own. Thus, my emphasis in my title that this interpretation of said verses of Thomas and Mary is my own - just as

Thomas and Mary may have been interpreting what they thought Jesus may have said.

Did Jesus really say what the Thomas and Mary of this work claimed he said? Who knows? But given that wisdom may be the underlying message of these verses, I think it is worthwhile to research the following verses as if Jesus - or a wise person or sage - may have offered them.

Was Jesus really a "lord" as "interpreters" Mark, Matthew, Luke, John, Peter, and Paul - among others - saw him? Or was he more of a "sage" than a "lord"? Indeed, that is the question; but this "interpreter" of life needs no "lord" as in some external person directing his life; and so my interpretation of Jesus must be the same. I do believe Jesus was indeed probably a "sage," but not a "lord."

How did Thomas and Mary see Jesus? As you will see in my upcoming interpretation of the verses from Thomas, I think Thomas saw Jesus as a "sage" too; and I think it is somewhat probable that Mary saw Jesus in the same light - though she does refer to Jesus as a "lord" - as you will see if you review my interpretation of The Gospel of Mary.

That interpretation only covers the 1st verse of The Gospel of Mary, however, because only the first verse deals with sayings of Jesus offered during his life. Subsequent verses of The Gospel of Mary deal with happenings after "Jesus left them;" and for this work - as in my previous work about The Gospel of Mary - I have little interest in what happened after "Jesus left them" because whatever happened did not deal with the sayings of Jesus - but rather with how various disciples or students saw Jesus after "he left them." I will leave others to ponder about that.

Be that as it may, however, it is important to realize that this work is my own - based on my vision of life - just as any interpretation must be an author's own - based on his or her own vision of life.

I wrote the works included in this compilation in 2009. It is now 2017. Has my interpretation - or interpretations - changed in that time? Maybe a little, but not so much that I need to alter my interpretations of 2009 - which are really about the same as my earlier interpretation of some of the verses as found in a 2003 writing I did called JESUS - A DIFFERENT VIEW.

Enough for this Introduction to this entire work. Each of my major writings of 2009 included in this volume will have their own Introduction. I will leave it at that. Enjoy the verses to be presented on their own merit - such as it is - and my interpretation of them by my own merit - such as it is. OK?

It is worth noting, however, that all of the works of this book can be found in Volume 7 of my *OUT IN THE OPEN* feature of my writing website - *www.una-bella-vita.com*. That *OUT IN THE OPEN* feature presents most of my writings from 1963 - 2012 in a chronological order - or in an order in which they were written. Check any of that out as you wish - along with various blogs added since the inception of my website in 2012. Also, refer to the end of this work for other works that I have published.

Also, I will be "throwing" in a few (8) songs I have written in the past, concluding with one I call *"The Same"* - which was written in September of 2008 - just one year prior to my writing my commentaries on the Gospels of Thomas & Mary. I like song a lot because one can express in verse that which is somewhat difficult to say in prose. *God Bless The Poet! - Even one like me!* As it is so often expressed in the net world - LOL! (Lots of Laughs)

Thanks!

Francis William Bessler (born: 12/3/1941)
Laramie, Wyoming
1/17/2017

Contents

Sense of Belonging

By
Francis William Bessler
Laramie, Wyoming
1/15/2009

REFRAIN:
I've a sense of belonging.
Longing is not my verse.
I've a sense of belonging;
and I belong to the Universe.
I've a sense of belonging.
I've belonged since my birth.
I've a sense of belonging;
and I belong to the Universe.

I'm no different than anyone;
but I admit to the truth.
Everyone here is equally dear –
regardless of age or youth.
If love is only a sense of belonging,
why is it that love we often evade
by deluding ourselves we must seek to belong
when we already belong to what's great?
Refrain.

We cannot make ourselves great
by thinking we're better than sheep or dogs.
If we do fall into that trap,
our penalty is a sense we don't belong.
I believe each part is wondrous,
as wondrous as the whole
because whatever is in the whole
must in each part also rule.
Refrain.

If I were to meet you in public
and you were to slap me in the face,
it would be best for me to walk away
and not repeat your mistake.
Today, someone died.
Tomorrow, it may be me;
but it's good to keep in mind
death does not lessen Divinity.
Refrain.

So, let us all be strong.
There's no need to be weak
because, in fact, we all belong
to Creation's Grand University.
Yes, in fact, we all belong
to God's Grand University.
Refrain.

FINAL:
I've a sense of belonging
and I'll belong even after this birth
because no matter where I may be,
I'll be within the Universe.
Yes, I've a sense of belonging
and I'll belong even after this birth
because no matter where I may be,
I'll be within the Universe.
Yes, I'll be within the Universe.
There's no escaping it –
I'll always belong – to and within –
the Universe.

Jesus Via Thomas Commentaries

§

By
Francis William Bessler
Laramie, Wyoming
- 2009 -

Introduction

§

WHO WAS THOMAS? IT SEEMS he was a man who took some notes a long time ago about a man named *Jesus*. Or maybe he jotted down his recollections long after Jesus died. I do not know anything about the details of what has become known as *THE GOSPEL ACCORDING TO THOMAS*. I am not a scholar of the languages or of history in any way. My reading of the Gospel of Thomas is almost strictly personal – approaching its verses from a viewpoint of my own rationale for life. That is to say, I suppose, that I may be *reading into* the Gospel of Thomas as much as I am *reading from* or *extracting from*.

Having admitted that, let me tell you what I do know about The Gospel of Thomas. I know that only recently in historical terms has it become known to modern man. In 1945, a peasant in Egypt stumbled onto a jar in a cave overlooking the Nile River in Egypt near a place or town or settlement known as Nag Hammadi. It was entirely an accident. Our peasant stumbled on some rather big ancient jar that contained a lot of stuff. When he overturned that jar, among some other ancient hidden works, out tumbled

THE GOSPEL ACCORDING TO THOMAS – or at least the first 114 verses of a work that may have included more than those 114 verses; but it is my understanding that only the first 114 were recoverable.

From carbon dating, as I understand it, the age of the contents of this jar could be traced to around the 4th Century. What happened in the 4th Century that prompted stuffing things in a jar and hiding the jar in a cave dwelling off the Nile River? In general, an Emperor named Constantine who had just taken over the Western World and had decided to make Christianity the state religion. He wanted unity in his empire and he did not like conflict about his new hero, Jesus. There were lots of gospels in his empire about Jesus, but they did not all tell the same story. He wanted the same story to be told to all and obeyed by all. So he felt it necessary to select only those gospels that told a somewhat favorable story and outlaw the rest. He commanded his bishops to set-tle on a canon – and *THE HOLY BIBLE* was born out of that. Of course, this *BIBLE* included lots of books, other than just gospels about Jesus, but around 325 or so, it was born by command of Constantine.

Among the many books excluded from the new canon was *THE GOSPEL ACCORDING TO THOMAS*, as well as another of my favorites, *THE GOSPEL OF MARY.* I offer my interpretation of The Gospel of Mary in another work – **JESUS VIA MARY COMMENTARIES** - but this is a work about The Gospel of Thomas. Constantine (and/or his bishops) decided that any gospels not selected for the new canon should not only be excluded from the new **BIBLE,** but banned from the public as well. Thus, as I understand it, all "outlaw" works were to be destroyed.

Fortunately, some monks (or monk) disobeyed the order to destroy all copies of banned works and did what they could to hide them away for posterity. That is why ***THE GOSPEL ACCORDING TO THOMAS (THE GOSPEL OF THOMAS)*** was put in a jar and hidden away in a cave for safe keeping. If those mindful monks (or monk) had not done that, we would have no alternate gospel to talk about today and Matthew, Mark, Luke, and John would remain sole custodians of Jesus.

Due to the disobedience of someones or one, however, Matthew, Mark, Luke, and John are no longer sole custodians of Jesus. After all these years of having to keep quiet, others who offered different stories about Jesus are finally being heard. **The Ban of Constantine is Over!**

THE GOSPEL ACCORDING TO THOMAS found in 1945 was written in Coptic, an Egyptian Language. It may have been written originally in Greek, but the copy found in 1945 was an Egyptian translation. It is largely held by so called experts that the author, Thomas, was likely Thomas, one of the original apostles of Jesus. Supposedly, Thomas was Greek. So it stands to reason that he would have written an original in Greek. Who knows what happened to the original Greek? Perhaps it did not survive its pre Constantine days – and perhaps it was in the care of some obedient monk who did as he was told and burned it as contraband.

The Gospel of Thomas only contains a series of *Jesus said* statements. There is no narrative offered – just a bunch of *Jesus said* statements. I get the feeling that Thomas may have actually taken notes during the life of Jesus and this gospel may be the result of his jottings. You may get that sense too as you review the verses. Imagine a student taking notes – as primitive as that would have been in 30 A.D. But people did write in those days and manuscripts were written on papyrus or whatever. So it is feasible someone could have taken notes during the life of Jesus.

If so, those notes in the form of **THE GOSPEL ACCORDING TO THOMAS** may have been the first writings about Jesus. Others like Peter's boys – Matthew, Mark, Luke, and John – could have started with those writings and then expounded stories from there – stories both true and false. Given the apparent disagreement between the Jesus reflected in the Gospel of Thomas and the other gospels, it could have happened in just that way. In reality, Thomas may have been the favorite of Jesus for being the more understanding companion and Peter may have been a man looking for a cause and seeing one in Jesus.

In any case, in time, after the discovery in 1945, scholars of Coptic have translated The Gospel of Thomas into various languages, including my own English. In 1979, I acquired my first copy; and I believe that translation may have been among the first of the English translations, if not the first. It was done by a team headed by a fellow named **A. Guillaumont** and was copyrighted in 1959. My copy included the Coptic on the left hand side of the book and the English translation on the right. Thus, if one knew both Coptic and English, one could refer between the languages, but being ignorant of Coptic myself, I read only the English pages on the right.

Unfortunately, I no longer have my original copy of Mr. Guillaumont's translation. After copying all the verses into a pc file for my own safe keeping, as strange as it seems to me, I lost my original copy. It is my copy of my own recording of the verses of The Gospel of Thomas that I feature in this work. I tried my best to copy the verses exactly as Mr. Guillaumont offered them in his translation, including all parentheses and brackets and little arrows where they were found. In some cases, I guess the team of translators could not decipher a word or expression and they had to guess about a word, but when they did guess, they made it clear that some word or expression was hard to decipher by punctuating their translations with marks that indicated some confusion.

Personally, I appreciate the integrity and honesty of a team of translators who will admit to confusion. I have read several "translations" that offer no confusion at all and recite verses like that is just as they were found. That often leaves the false impression that there was no confusion in the first place. If someone reads such a translation, they have no way of knowing that a verse may not be quite what it seems because a "translator" may have been no more than an "interpreter" of a previous translation and simply stated a personal opinion in the place of an authentic text.

Be that as it may, though Mr. Guillaumont did not explain his markings in his work of 1959, you will have them as best as I could reproduce them with my pc, using Microsoft Word. Most importantly, however, I think you will have as authentic a translation of The Gospel of Thomas as there is. You can judge the verses and my attending interpretation of those verses as you wish.

For what it's worth, as implied previously, I think it is highly possible – and maybe even probable – that the stories of Jesus as offered in the Gospels of Matthew, Mark, Luke, and John are far from complete – and maybe even misleading. I get the sense from the canon gospels that all the apostles of Jesus were in agreement that Jesus intended to present himself as a Jewish Messiah – or The Jewish Messiah; however I do not get such a sense from the Gospel of Thomas. In fact, I get the impression that Jesus wanted nothing to do with being part of Jewish history, let alone be its Messiah.

A messiah – or the notion of messiah – implies a belief in a separation between God and man. If there is no separation between God and man, then there is no need for a messiah to bond them. As I read both the Gospels of Thomas and Mary, I see a ***Holistic Jesus*** rather than a

Messianic Jesus. A *Holistic Jesus* is a Jesus who believes that life is whole as it is and needs no saving grace to make it whole. A **Messianic Jesus** is a Jesus who believes that life is not whole as it is and is in need of some saving grace to bond it with a God with which it has been previously separated.

Personally, I cannot reconcile the notion of infinite – which I think God is – with the traditional notion of sin. If God is infinite, that means God must be everywhere. If God is everywhere – and in everything – how is it possible for there to be a separation between God and anything? If there can be no real separation between God and man, then the Jewish notion of sin has to be wrong. If the Jewish notion of sin is wrong in that there never has been a separation between man and God, then the Jewish notion of messiah must also be wrong. A Jewish messiah is supposedly needed to reconcile man with God; but if there is no actual separation, neither is there need of reconciliation. Accordingly, Jesus must have another meaning other than that of Jewish Messiah.

It just so happens that both Thomas and Mary present a completely different perspective of Jesus than that offered by the canon gospels. The Jesus of Thomas and Mary seems to reject the notions of Judaism as related to sin. It is hard to believe. I know that. We have been led to believe for so long that Jesus believed that sin exists and that he was the one to resolve it in mankind. Now, we get the story – long suppressed by Constantine and history – that it was opinion offered in Matthew, Mark, Luke, and John – and not fact.

Certainly, Matthew, Mark, Luke, John, Peter, and Paul had a right to their opinions; but so did Thomas and Mary and all those who had various opinions about the man named Jesus. And speaking of opinions, this work is a set of my opinions based on my own personal interpretation of the verses offered for my use by the fine team, headed by A. Guillaumont. Make no mistake about it. That which you are about to review – and study if you wish – are the verses of Thomas as supplied by A. Guillaumont and team and my own opinions about their meaning.

I pride myself in being a student of life and Jesus. **That means I am still learning.** An interpretation of today might not be the same tomorrow. That is what happens when someone is a student. Their views change as their thoughts change. I wrote an interpretation of *THE GOSPEL ACCORDING TO THOMAS* in 2003 that remains for the most part my current interpretation, but there has been some changes. I will not detail the changes except to offer that there has been some. That is to emphasize that I am still a student and probably always will be. **I am still learning.**

I cannot stress how important a notion that is to me. I do not want anyone to assume that I know anything for sure. **I am only offering my opinion;** and I think that is what we should presume of Thomas and Mary and Matthew and Mark and Luke and John and Peter and Paul too. They did not know anymore than what I know today, but they had their opinions about things. As long as we approach any writing in that light, I think we can do ourselves a wonder of good, but when we approach any work like it is some definitive glossary of the meaning of life, that is when we are apt to stumble – and maybe stumble badly.

In my opinion, mankind is still very much in the dark about Jesus because Constantine and his bishops chose to exclude certain opinions and tried to make everyone believe some so called mainstream opinions as if those opinions were unquestionably right. Never in my wildest way would I ever submit that any of my opinions are unquestionably right. The very nature of opinion is that it may or may not be right. So to assume that anyone has a hold on what is unquestionably right is about as dumb a thing as we can do if we want to preserve our status as students of life.

In regard to any opinion about life, I think it is very useful to consider the person with the opinion. What is his general belief about life? What was Peter's general belief about life? What was John's general belief about life? What was Mark's general belief about life? What was Paul's general belief about life? What was Thomas's general belief about life? What was Mary Magdalene's general belief about life? What is Francis William Bessler's general belief about life?

Just as my approach to Jesus must be colored by my general belief about life, so it has to be with everyone. I mentioned at the outset that I may be **reading into *THE GOSPEL ACCORDING TO THOMAS*** with some of my prejudices and preconceived notions about things. Without question, I admit that; but so also does anyone who writes about or reviews a verse. We all do it. It comes with the territory of a **"general belief"** about life.

What was Peter's general belief about life? How did that color his perception of Jesus? I think Peter believed in the Jewish dogma that man and God are separated by virtue of some sin of Adam. If so, he could only review Jesus in that light. What about Thomas? Not much is known about him. Did he meet Jesus with a preconception about man being lost in sin? Perhaps yes. Perhaps not. If Thomas was Greek by origin – as he may have been – and was only visiting Israel when he met Jesus, he may not have been equipped with the Jewish notion of sin. If so, he could have heard a different Jesus – or he could have seen Jesus in a different way than did Peter. Thus, his opinion about Jesus would necessarily be different than that of Peter.

That is the way it goes. I get the impression from the Gospel of Thomas that Jesus was not very impressed with Peter. That may be because Thomas was not very impressed with Peter. Who is to say? I get the impression that Matthew, Mark, Luke, and John and Paul were all impressed with Peter. Maybe they were so because of sharing a general belief about life. Maybe they all met Jesus with a preconceived notion of sin in hand whereas Thomas may have been without such a preconception.

The point of all this is to emphasize that all of this is opinion. To assume that the opinions of Peter and his boys are somehow inspired of God and the opinions of Thomas and Mary are without useful inspiration is truly foolish. To declare that the **BIBLE** in general is inspired of God and this set of commentaries is not is about as defeating as you can get. It is probably because some men have decided that they deserve to be anointed with inspiration and others anointed with desperation that man has been at war for all of his days on this Earth so far.

Make no mistake. I am of God, but am no more inspired of God than anyone else. Of course, that is an opinion. I see God as infinite and in everything and everything emanating from God. That is my **general belief** about life. It is that belief that I take with me everywhere I go and it is that belief that I use to judge the wisdom or folly of anything in life. Peter and his subordinates, Matthew, Mark, Luke and John did not possess that same **general belief**. Accordingly, they could not decide about any issue in life in the same way as I do – or you do or as Jesus did or does.

With that, let us take a look at the opinions of a man named Thomas as he jotted them down over 2,000 years ago. He saw Jesus in a different way than did Peter and his subordinates because he was possessed with a different **general belief** about life than they. Maybe you will agree with how Thomas is perceiving Jesus and maybe not. Maybe you will agree with how I am perceiving both Thomas and Jesus – and maybe not.

In any case, I am happy I can share with you how I see it. I may be wrong. I have been wrong in the past. That is as definite a proof as one needs that I may be wrong now too. On the other hand, I am not new at reviewing the verses of *THE GOSPEL ACCORDING TO THOMAS*. I have been meditating on these verses since 1979 – when I encountered them for the first time. With all that meditation, maybe I am close to the truth – at least much closer than I was in 1979 and a little bit closer than I was in 2003 when I wrote my first full interpretation of The Gospel of Thomas. That one I called **JESUS – A DIFFERENT VIEW.**

In 2005, I met with a number of interested students of The Gospel of Thomas on a weekly basis for twenty-three weeks. Those sessions clarified my thinking a bit; and it is largely because of that clarification that I decided to offer a whole new interpretation. We students can do that. **It is only those who refuse to change that cannot see their way clear to embrace anything new; and in their defiance of change, they refuse to correct error and remain as blind as they were yesterday.** That is just the way it is.

One final note: In this work, I am most intent on sharing the verses of *THE GOSPEL ACCORDING TO THOMAS* and not my personal interpretation of those verses. My personal interpretation is not so important; but sharing the verses themselves is. Hopefully you will take the verses and formulate your own interpretation of them. If you wish, you can even skip over my interpretation and ponder only the verses themselves on your own.

Finally, my eternal thanks to the team of **A. Guillaumont** for providing the translation of the verses as they have – an effort copyrighted in 1959.

Sincerely,
Francis William Bessler
April 12th, 2009

Beginning:
These are the secret words which the Living
Jesus spoke
and Didymos Judas Thomas wrote.

Verse 1:
And He said: Whoever finds the explanation
of these words will not taste death.

Tasting death is fearing death, not experiencing it. It is living in fear of death and what may come afterward. Whoever finds the explanation of these words will have wisdom and will not fear death anymore than they will fear life. Life and death are part of a continuum. To know one is to not fear the other. Death only continues life. It does not end it. So what is to fear about death – unless that which is in life now is not desired to be continued after death? If we do not want to continue as we are, then we better change what we are – or how we are – because death will not stop what goes before. It is only like an intermission between one life and the next.

Verse 2:
Jesus said: Let him who seeks, not cease seeking until he finds, and when he finds, he will be troubled, and when he has been troubled, he will marvel and he will reign over the All.

Essentially, Jesus offered that we should seek until we find. He added that when we find – the answers for which we seek – we will be troubled. I think that is because the answers we seek are probably contrary to what most think is the truth. It is indeed troubling to face the possibility that we have not been living the truth. It was true when Jesus lived and it is still true today.

What does Jesus mean by *"reign over the All"*? He offered that when we have found the truths for which we seek, we will marvel and reign over the All? What did he mean by that? Good question; but I think the key to "reign" is in the word "marvel." By marveling what we know and see, we will reign over the All – or better perhaps – **with the All**. To know ourselves as the *"sons* *of the Living Father"* as is offered in the next verse is to marvel at what we know because the reality is so amazing. If we truly find ourselves, we can only marvel about what we find – and it is in marveling about what we find that makes us like kings. It is not in commanding others that we are kings. It is in marveling about the truths of life that we find security – which is what being part of a "kingdom" is all about. Right?

Verse 3:
Jesus said: If those who lead you say to you: "See, the Kingdom is in heaven", then the birds of the heaven will precede you. If they say to you: "It is in the sea," then the fish will precede you. But the Kingdom is within you and it is without you. If you (will) know yourselves, then you will be known and you will know that you are the sons of the Living Father. But if you do not know yourselves, then you are in poverty and you are poverty.

Jesus offered that we should not be fooled if someone tells us that Heaven - The Kingdom - is over here or over there. He said that the Kingdom is inside of us and outside of us and that if we would only realize it, we are *"sons of the Living Father."* Amazingly, traditional Christianity would have us believe that Jesus is the **"only son of God."** The

Jesus of Thomas tells us in the Gospel of Thomas that we are all sons of God - or children of God. It is one of the great errors of traditional Christianity that Jesus was the only son of God when, in truth, he was only a son of God - along with the rest of us.

In offering that the Kingdom is within us and without us – or outside of us – that pretty much says "everywhere." Doesn't it? Many have the idea that the Kingdom (of Peace) is elsewhere and that after life we may find it, but Jesus is arguing here that the Kingdom we may think is elsewhere is right here and right now. If we do not know that, then we act without awareness and are ignorant – or as Jesus offers, are in poverty. We who act like God is not already inside us are poor because we lack the riches of wisdom. If we realize that God is everywhere, then we would act accordingly. We would know we are *"sons of the Living Father"* – or children of the same.

In a very real way, we are the Living Father because we come from Him or It. We have to be sons of the Living Father because anything that comes from the Living Father has to be part of the Living Father. That makes us all sons. "Son" here is not saying "masculine." It is only saying "like God." A "son" is like his "father." If we are from God, we are "like God" because we are made in the likeness of God. But that is not just we who are human. That is everything in Creation because everything that is created comes from God. How can we not marvel about that?

Verse 4:
Jesus said: The man old in days will not hesitate to ask a little child of seven days about the place of Life, and he will live. For many who are first shall become last and they shall become a single one.

I think Jesus was arguing here that life is continuous. **The old becomes the new, but the new only extends as a continuation of the old.** Personally, I think Jesus believed in reincarnation and there will be verses that imply that beside this one, but even without incarnation, whatever comes after is only a continuation of what went before. A "child of seven days" represents the new – a beginning of a new life. "Old in days" represents the end of life – the old. When Jesus says "for many who are first will become last," it is only a way of saying that what is last will become first.

Last is old. First is new. But, as he says, they shall become a single one. That is to say, the new will continue in the same mold as the old. The new soul will be reborn, as it were, but will only continue the paths of a former existence. That is really the true nature of judgment. Lots have in mind that judgment is being punished by someone outside of ourselves, but I think Jesus realized it is not punishment from without, but continuation from within. If that does not tell us to get it right so that we do not have to continue the wrong, nothing will.

Verse 5:
Jesus said: Know what is in thy sight, and what is hidden from thee will be revealed to thee. For there is nothing hidden that will not be manifest.

There is tremendous depth in this one. It is one of my favorite quotes of all time. It says so much. ***"Know what is in thy sight"*** tells us to know our lives, know about them, know them inside and out, know ourselves. It is to say that which is knowable is worthy of being known. **To know in a spiritual sense is to become one with, to have a sense of union.** You cannot know something or someone and not be part of them. Knowledge of self leads to knowledge of others. Ignorance of self leads to ignorance of others.

I am not sure that the word "revealed" is a good word for what Jesus is trying to say here, but in essence, he is saying that if we know what we can see, we can experience what we can't see. Perhaps the better word would be "inexperienced" in place of "hidden." What is hidden is really that which is inexperienced. He is offering that we can "experience" or "know" that which we can't see – God – by knowing and appreciating what we can see. That makes sense. If God is making us – as I think Jesus believed – then we can "experience" God by loving that which God is making – us. We are a manifestation of God. We are a manifestation of the hidden God.

Lots think that they can know God as God is, but no one who is finite can know that which is infinite. God is infinite. **We will never know God "face to face" on the same level; but we can know God by knowing and loving that which God is making – us.** Pretty simple, huh?

Verse 6:
His disciples asked Him, they said to Him: Wouldst thou that we fast, and how should we pray, (and) should we give alms, and what diet should we observe? Jesus said: Do not lie; and do not do what you hate, for all things are manifest before Heaven. For there is nothing hidden that shall not be revealed and there is nothing covered that shall remain without being uncovered.

What a verse this one is! When asked if they should fast and give alms, one would have thought that Jesus would have encouraged doing just that for the sake of the soul; but our Jesus of Thomas did not so much as tell his disciples not to fast and give alms and pray, but that none of those things are important; though in one of the following verses (Verse 14), he does say don't do these things because doing them will actually hurt you spiritually. **Telling the truth and respecting the truth is all that is important for the soul.**

Why would Jesus suggest that praying is not very useful? Because generally one prays to a God outside of him or herself. Jesus knew that God is not outside of us for us to have to pray for Him or It or Her to come to us. If I pray to God with the hope that God is going to do something for me as a result of my prayer, then I am ignoring that God is already inside of me. If we pray, I suppose we should pray to only those outside of us - like perhaps saints or angels. It may be just fine to pray to that kind, but to pray to a God Which is inside of you does not make a whole lot of sense. Does it?

Then Jesus adds that there is nothing hidden that shall not be revealed, for all things are manifest before Heaven. Seems like we already covered that idea in the previous verse, but I think it is to say that spiritually we can't fool the truth. We can pretend that we are something we are not in this world that we see, but in the world of spirit, our real thoughts and attitudes are what judge us. We can't stay hidden in a spiritual sense because our real attitudes and spirits judge us. Like I mentioned in a previous verse, I don't think any of us should concern ourselves with judgment from another upon us. I think we should only be concerned about being in tune with ourselves - or we should care about ourselves being in tune with the things that really matter like the attitude of equality of being.

Verse 7:
Jesus said: Blessed is the lion which the man eats and the lion will become man; and cursed is the man whom the lion eats and the lion will become man.

I think it only means that blessed is the one who is angry who is converted by one who is at peace. The lion stands for something fierce or angry and the man stands for one at peace - in this verse at least. Cursed am I if I allow someone who is not at peace to convert me to his angry or hateful ways. That is all Jesus is saying here.

I think this is one of the clearest dictations, as it were, that it is not smart to become a soldier to oppose a soldier. Jesus would not agree with that stance. Thus, he could not approve of war because to go to war and be willing to kill another who may be out to kill me, I would have to become what I resent. That is allowing the lion to eat me and make me as it is. Not smart!

Verse 8:
And He said: The Man is like a wise fisherman who cast his net into the sea, he drew it up from the sea full of small fish; among them he found a large (and) good fish, that wise fisherman, he threw all the small fish down into the sea, he chose the large fish without regret. Whoever has ears to hear, let him hear.

If I am out fishing, why not catch the biggest fish I can? Jesus is only saying here that I should not settle for knowing less that I can. That is like catching only a small fish. I should be willing to throw all the little fishes away that represent being less than what I can be – and only settle for being the best that I can be. But as I think Jesus would argue, doing the best I can is not what it is all about. It is realizing that I am a *"son of the Living Father"* and acting accordingly – marveling at my existence and experiencing the hidden God through the unhidden me and the unhidden all that is.

Verse 9:

Jesus said: See, the sower went out, he filled his hand, he threw. Some (seeds) fell on the road; the birds came, they gathered them. Others fell on the rock and did not strike root in the earth and did not produce ears. And others fell on the thorns; they choked the seed and the worm ate them. And others fell on the good earth; and it brought forth good fruit; it bore sixty per measure and one hundred twenty per measure.

This is only telling it like it is. Some of us can hear an idea and grasp it and some cannot. **To be able to grasp an idea, one needs to prepare him or herself with good principle.** Otherwise, a good idea can go to waste.

It can fall among thorns or rocks and never grow. Ideas – and that is what Jesus is talking about here – require a good foundation to be understood.

I can tell you to **"do good"** and not prepare you with another idea that you are a *"son of the Living Father."* If you do not know you are a son of the Living Father, then the notion of "doing good" will probably go to waste. You won't have any idea what it means. Jesus is only saying here that to experience spiritual growth, we must first recognize some elementary truths. We must prepare ourselves with good earth and good principle. If we do not prepare ourselves with elementary truths, then any dictums that are issued that are dictums of wisdom may not be able to live within us; but if we are prepared for worthwhile ideas, then we can receive them and they will bear much fruit.

Verse 10:
Jesus said: I have cast fire upon the world, and see, I guard it until it (the world) is afire.

The truth hurts at first when you are unaccustomed to it. No one likes to confront the truth that he or she has been wrong. By offering that the world is not comprised of good and evil like the Jews believed and like so many still believe today, people of old could only resent the message rather than be comforted by it. The Jews found great comfort in the idea that they were a chosen people – that they were chosen to be "sons of the Living Father." Of course, that is pure nonsense. God does not choose some to be his sons and not all to be his sons. But if I am convinced that inequality is the basis of salvation and not equality, then I will be disturbed to hear otherwise.

Jesus came to disturb the world with the truth. That is all he is saying here. He is not talking in literal terms because he almost never talked in literal terms. The fire that he is casting upon the world is not real fire, but ideas that hurt because they confront us. In Verse 2, Jesus said: *Let him who seeks, not cease seeking until he finds, and when he finds, he will be troubled, and when he has been troubled, he will marvel and he will reign over the All.* It is that "being troubled" with confronting ideas that amounts to the fire he is casting upon the world. But, as he offers, the fire will not last if we deal with it. Once we overcome our being troubled, we will marvel at what we find anew and reign as a king – secure within our new ideas.

Verse 11:
Jesus said: This heaven shall pass away and the one above it shall pass away, and the dead are not alive and the living shall not die. In the days that you devoured the dead, you made it alive; when you come into the light, what will you do? On the day when you were one, you became two. But when you have become two, what will you do?

I think Jesus is offering that at some point, the world will end – as we know it now. Verse 111 addresses the end of the world too. When Jesus offers that *this heaven will pass away*, I think he is referring to what folks think of as "the sky." When he refers to *the one above it will pass away*, I think he is referring to the mythical heaven – the heaven that people think they are going to after death. If that mythical heaven "passes away," there goes the eternal heaven that many folks are counting on.

But why should that mythical heaven pass away? My guess is that it will pass away because it is really one with the regular sky and the regular Earth. That is to say that "heaven" is all caught up with life on Earth in some way. There may be no mythical heaven where souls go to rest for eternity after serving a life on Earth. There may only be the Earth and its heavenly status during life. What life? The life of the soul within the body – the life here and now.

At the end of the world, Jesus says *the dead are not alive and the living shall not die.* Knowing Jesus as I think I do and his focus on the kingdom of the Father being within us and without us – or outside of us – I think Jesus is referring to the "dead" as those who are not alive in this life– or not aware, though they are alive. Who can that be? Those who fail to understand that the kingdom of the Father is here and now. If one lives life unaware that the kingdom is now, then, in a very real way, that one is living a "dead" life in terms of being "unaware" of the life of plenty he or she actually has.

Life is probably very much defined for a soul in a body as being alive while within that body. People have some notion that life after the body will be a better life, but that is probably so only if the soul is reinvested in another body. But time may run out at least for some interim period where there is no more life on Earth and therefore, no bodies available to incarnate. In that event, souls will be left with their last state prior to their "last death" in a body. Of those, if a soul did not achieve awareness of the kingdom of the Father while alive, they will remain dead. Of those, if a soul did achieve awareness of the kingdom of the Father, they will remain alive – or aware.

What did Jesus mean when he said: ***in the days that you devoured the dead, you made it alive?*** I think he was talking about our taking in ideas. If we live our lives basing our lives on false ideas, then we are "devouring the dead." What may have been the false ideas he was talking about? Since he was talking to Jews, more than likely it would have been the false ideas of their tradition – namely that the kingdom of the Father is not at hand and is not for everyone. That would be my guess. We can "make alive" that which is really "dead" if we live according to dead or false ideas. I think that is what Jesus is offering here – warning us, in effect, that we better get things right while we have the chance because there will come a day when we will have no more chances.

On the day that you were one, you became two. What did he mean by that? Two stands for "confusion" in this text. So Jesus is offering that if we become one with something false, then we become confused. I think he was referring once again to the notion of being one with the falsity of Jewish tradition. If I am in alignment with a false notion, I am one with that notion. The same, of course, could be said about being in alignment with a true notion. I am also one with that notion; but Jesus is not talking about right notions here. He is warning against the false ones because he offers that *when you have become two, what will you do?* When you have become confused believing in the false notion that the kingdom of the Father is not here and now, what will you do? Your confusion will continue. How could it be otherwise if resolving confusion is being aware of the kingdom of the Father while in the body? If you no longer have a body, as the "end of the world" implies, you will have no more chance to get it right and become aware that the kingdom of the Father is here and now. Jesus is only warning us here that we have just so much time to get it right because the world will end at some point and we will be left with our last states of mind.

From an evolutionary standpoint, life may regenerate on Earth after an eon of time and incarnation of bodies by souls may resume, but in that interim that life has ceased on Earth – probably more for cosmic happenings than for any other reason – perhaps when the Earth will go into another long ice age – there will be no life on Earth and therefore, no chances of incarnation. It might happen that way.

Verse 12:
The disciples said to Jesus: We know that thou wilt go away from us. Who is it who shall be great over us? Jesus said to them: Wherever you have come, you will go to James the righteous for whose sake heaven and earth came into being.

Who knows who James the righteous was and what Jesus may have meant when he said that heaven and Earth came into being for the sake of James the righteous? My first guess is that James represents the same providence of souls that Jesus represented. From the standpoint of both Jesus and James, Planet Earth is useful for their purpose. Therefore, it came into being in a way for their sake.

But everyone could say the same thing. Anyone who is on Earth could be here for his or her own purpose. That might be stretching it, but I think it is so. I think that various communities of souls incarnate on Earth for various reasons. So, it would not be fair to say that the Earth only exists for the incarnation of souls from soulful communities like those of James and Jesus; but it would be fair to say that James and Jesus have chosen the Earth for their purpose. And what is that purpose? To instruct others that the kingdom of the Father is here and now and for everyone. Such awareness is the best way for a soul to prepare for any existence of peace – be it within a body or outside of a body.

Verse 13:

Jesus said to His disciples: Make a comparison to Me and tell Me whom I am like. Simon Peter said to Him: Thou art like a righteous angel. Matthew said to Him: Thou art like a wise man of understanding. Thomas said to Him: Master, my mouth will not at all be capable of saying whom Thou art like. Jesus said: I am not thy Master, because thou hast drunk, thou hast become drunk from the bubbling spring which I have measured out. And He took him, He withdrew, he spoke three words to him. Now when Thomas came to his companions, they asked him: What did Jesus say to thee? Thomas said to them: If I tell you one of the words which He said to me, you will take up stones and throw at me; and the fire will come from the stones and burn you up.

Just by offering that Thomas should not see Jesus as a "master," much is offered in this verse that tends to contradict the traditional image of Jesus as lord - if by lord is meant ruler or supervisor. I do believe the traditional understanding of "lord" is "ruler." Given that understanding of lord (or master), in this verse, I hear Jesus practically begging Thomas not to see him in that light. The reason is that no one of wisdom even begins to want to be a ruler.

Lords want to be rulers - or at least think they deserve to be so; but true wise souls like Jesus have no attraction toward wanting to be rulers or lords. A truly wise person only wants another person to share a personal vision or intellectual or spiritual impression of life so as to know freedom on his or her own merit.

One who is free - such as was Jesus - can only remain free if no one actually depends on him for their virtue. This is what so many who misunderstand Jesus lack. They think that Jesus wants them to be hangers on as if Jesus will be pleased if they call him lord. I can assure you if someone called me 'lord,' I would quickly try to dissuade them because I would know great disappointment that the other does not know his or her own virtue. If it takes one to know one, being anti-lord myself, I can't imagine anyone wanting to bear such a burden. It would be alright if in bearing the burden, another gained needed insight to become his or her own master; but how could anyone gain such insight by holding on to a belief that he or she is deficient? It is quite a question. Isn't it? All I can say is that I do not envy Jesus for his having to put up with such a cockeyed misunderstanding of him as to even begin to think of him as a lord or master of another.

What were the three words that Jesus spoke to Thomas that if revealed to Peter and Matthew would anger them – as in the reference that *fire will come from the stones and burn you up*? That is a good question. I do not know what they might be specifically, but in general something like:

Don't be fooled, meaning do not be fooled by Peter and Matthew who are looking for the kingdom of the Father outside themselves. In other words, Jesus could have recognized that Peter was not getting it, so to speak, and that he, Thomas, ought to be careful to not be misled by Peter and Matthew because of their misunderstanding of him, Jesus. I suspect that is the proper meaning of this verse. In essence, the three words were **"Beware of Peter."**

Of course, we know from the other gospels that Peter would go forward to claim that Jesus chose him to lead his new church. Peter would go forward to teach Jesus as lord and not merely teacher – just the opposite of what Jesus wanted. Jesus offers here that when we listen to his ideas, they become our own and we become our own lords or masters - but only over ourselves. **It is the bubbling spring of ideas that set us free, not any one person, be it a Jesus or otherwise.**

Verse 14:

Jesus said to them: If you fast, you will beget sin for yourselves, and if you pray, you will be condemned, and if you give alms, you will do evil to your spirits. And if you go into any land and wander in the regions, if they receive you, eat what they set before you, heal the sick among them. For what goes into your mouth will not defile you, but what comes out of your mouth, that is what will defile you.

Imagine Jesus warning against praying. At first glance, it would seem absurd. But prefacing this warning with the counsel in verse 13 about becoming your own master by virtue of hearing the right ideas and attending to them, praying to God as if God is outside of me could only harm my soul. Why? Because it impresses upon myself a lie that God is not already inside of me. We covered this in previous verses, but I don't think it can be over emphasized. **If I am praying to impress a God that I think is outside of me, but which is actually inside of me, then I am leaving myself wide open to a misunderstanding of life on my part and also open to some potential meddling into my affairs by souls without bodies who may just be waiting to hear an appeal from a soul such as me.** If I pray to God, thinking that he or she who is hearing me is God, then I am leaving myself wide open to being manipulated by some bodiless agent who may be more than happy to present him or herself as the God I think I am addressing. Not smart! As Jesus would say, let him who has ears hear!

Jesus offers that what goes into our mouths does not defile us, but rather that which comes out of our mouths. What goes into our mouths? Food. The Jews were of the idea that certain foods are not pure – like pork – but Jesus is offering here that we cannot defile ourselves by what we eat. We can only defile ourselves by what we think and what we speak. We speak what we think; and it is in speaking foolish thoughts that we defile ourselves.

Verse 15:
Jesus said: When you see Him who was not born of woman, prostrate yourselves upon your face and adore Him: He is your Father.

I think Jesus is only offering here that our true parent of soul is not a person as such that we can see. None of us has a human body for a parent of our soul. Our souls are born of other stuff, so to speak. Jesus is not so much denigrating our humanity by offering that none of our souls are born of flesh as he is offering that we should be aware that our true soulful heritage may not be what it might seem. Of course we can't see our true soulful parent - or parents; but if we could, we should be ready to prostrate ourselves in front of him or her or it and offer thanks because without that parentage - whatever it may be - we would not be as souls.

Verse 16:
Jesus said: Men possibly think that I have come to throw peace upon the world and they do not know that I have come to throw divisions upon the earth, fire, sword, war. For there shall be five in a house: three shall be against two and two against three, the father against the son, and the son against the father, and they will stand as solitaries.

We often think that peace is something that can be delivered to the world. It is not. Peace has to be earned, I think. Peace only happens when souls realize a sense of fulfillment; but fulfillment is not something that can happen except with self-esteem. Jesus came into a world that was of the mind that a messiah can bring peace by virtue of some messianic power in itself. To suggest that peace is not a social or communal thing – as was expected – but an individual thing, such a message could only divide people. **Those who expected that peace can be delivered to a community or nation by virtue of God acting on behalf of that community or nation could only become upset with a man who would challenge a favored nation concept of salvation.** Thus, father would be turned against son and son against father. In the light of such divisiveness, peace for many would be illusive.

What does Jesus mean by *they will stand as solitaries*? I think it is only to mean that each of us is alone in regard to really achieving peace in our lives. I cannot gain peace for you, nor can you gain peace for me. Each of us must pursue and attain peace strictly as solitary souls, independent of all outside of us; but regardless of our achieving peace or not, in the end, each soul truly stands alone. Standing as solitaries, however, would also apply to two or more being in unison – regardless of motive or vision.

Verse 17:

Jesus said: I will give you what eye has not seen and what ear has not heard and what hand has not touched and (what) has not arisen in the heart of man.

I think Jesus is only offering here that he has a wisdom that is unusual – or was unusual for the times. Most of the Jews of the time were expecting salvation by virtue of a national blessing. Just in offering that salvation is strictly a personal thing not tied to national identity, Jesus was offering to those Jews ideas that had *"not arisen in the heart of man."* It should be very comforting indeed that my salvation is strictly up to me and not dependent upon my obeying some external law imposed upon me from without. Even today, however, many do not see salvation except in the light of a reward by another, that other being an external God. Even today, for so many, Jesus still represents what *"has not arisen in the heart of man."* Even today, many men do not get it. **Salvation is strictly a matter of personal disposition, not reward from without.**

Verse 18:

The disciples said to Jesus: Tell us how our end will be. Jesus said: Have you then discovered the beginning so that you inquire about the end? For where the beginning is, there shall be the end. Blessed is he who shall stand at the beginning, and he shall know the end and he shall not taste death.

For me, Jesus is offering a tale of reincarnation here. **It is to say that where the ending is, the beginning of something else is.** Blessed are we if we can position ourselves at our beginning - in my opinion, birth into a body - and look forward to a repeat performance upon death - being born again. I do not know about you, but when I do just that, it leaves me with no fear of death. I know that death is only a portal to a new life. And what a wonderful notion it is too - to know that the new baby I will be will be dependent like a new child on the old me - the parent of the child to be. Yes, that would say that I am my own parent - or the parent of the child to be. Nice thought, huh?

Verse 19:
Jesus said: Blessed is he who was before he came into being. If you become disciples to Me and hear My words, these stones will minister to you. For you have five trees in Paradise, which are unmoved in summer (or) in winter and their leaves do not fall. Whoever knows them will not taste death.

Wow! This one is chuck full of wisdom. Where do I begin? First, Jesus is offering, I think, that blessed am I if I am aware of the process. **Blessed am I if I am aware that I was before and will be again.** The wonder of this blessing is that it puts total responsibility on myself "to get it right" or "to get me right." If I live unaware that I was before, then I will probably live like I don't have to be after I am too. That leaves me open to all sort of bad guidance because others will be quick to inform me, teach me, command me, that some unknown has something in store for me - depending on how I act in life. Thus, the proverbial threat of Heaven if I am good and Hell if I am bad. If I am aware that I was before I came into being and will be after I am, then I am not likely to fall for the threats and decisions and regulations of others. I am my own soul. It is for me to determine who I am - and who I will be.

Then Jesus said, ***if you become disciples to Me, and hear My words, these stones will administer to you.*** Who knows the exact language that was offered, but in general I think it offers that **if - like Jesus - I become aware that I am an equal part of life, that equality - in terms of being aware of the divinity (Divinity) of all - will make it seem as if anything that exists is my brother - or friend.** Friends administer to one another. Thus, even a stone, full of the blessedness of divinity will be a friend and an administrator to me.

If you doubt this, then take a moment to sit on a hill on a quiet day when nothing else is about to disturb you. Look about. If it is for you like it is for me, I become part of all my surroundings. I can reach down and grab a stone and study it, touch it, embrace it, kiss it, rub it up against me - and that stone becomes like my best friend. I think this is what Jesus is offering. To be like him is to have everything as a friend - even a dead stone.

Then he said that there are *five trees in Paradise that are unmoved in summer or winter and whose leaves do not fall.* If I know those five trees of Paradise, then I will not taste death. I think he is offering that no. 1, Paradise is here and now - depending on some awareness if the threat of death can not keep me from it - and no. 2, if I find that Paradise, I will not taste death.

I think he is offering that I should not let death scare me if I love the process. Death is part of the process. **To be aware of the process and embrace it is to not fear it - at least when the process is so grand as life and death really are.** It is really life before death, then death, then life again – in a body, that is. The soul simply continues through all of it. So what is to fear about that?

About the five trees, though the author of this verse may have been relating to some magic to the number 5 of which I am unaware, being unaware of that magic, I can only take it to mean something like the 5 senses. The 5 senses are unmoved in summer and winter in that they happen regardless of season. Right? They keep on regardless of season and are therefore not tied to the seasons. Being aware of the wonder and the divinity of my 5 senses allows me to live life fully. **The key is to know those 5 senses are Divine and Good and of God or in God - or that God is in them.** This is Paradise - and it can be had right now, right here. Make sense?

Verse 20:
The disciples said to Jesus: Tell us what the Kingdom of Heaven is like. He said to them: It is like a mustard-seed, smaller than all seeds. But when it falls on the tilled earth, it produces a large branch and becomes shelter for <the> birds of heaven.

I think Jesus is offering here that the Kingdom of Heaven is the result of a very small seed. We tend to think that Heaven is due to some magnanimous happening or event when it is really due to a very small idea – or an idea that is very easy to understand, without complication. **That little idea is that "the kingdom of the Father is already here."** It is a very small idea, but that idea is like a huge tree that provides shelter for those who heed it and are nourished by it.

Verse 21:
Mary said to Jesus: Whom are thy disciples like? He said: They are like little children who have installed themselves in a field which is not theirs. When the owners of the field come, they will say: "Release to us our field". They take off their clothes before them to release it (the field) to them and to give back their field to them. Therefore I say: If the lord of the house knows that the thief is coming,

he will stay awake before he comes and will not let him dig through into his house of his kingdom to carry away his goods. You then must watch for the world, gird up your loins with great strength lest the brigands find (a) way to come to you, because they will find the advantage which you expect. Let there be among you a man of understanding; when the fruit ripened, he came quickly with his sickle in his hand, he reaped it. Whoever has ears to hear, let him hear.

Wow! Does this say a lot. At least my take on it is that Jesus is offering that his disciples are ones who are not understanding his true message and are trying to take him and make him what he is not. They have installed themselves in a field that is not theirs, I think, is to say that they are out of line with what he is trying to offer in terms of how he thought they were seeing him; and he was probably right. **They were expecting a real lord; and he was only, in truth, a sage - a wise man.**

Who knows what the initial word "disciple" was in the original language of the gospel? It may have been changed from some word meaning "follower" to the more favorable word "disciple" to imply that those who called themselves disciples really knew what Jesus was about. Mary may have had some "followers" of Jesus in mind that she was referencing and a translator may have interpreted an initial "follower" as "disciple." Who knows about that? But whatever the case - be it some known followers or disciples - I think **Jesus felt they were out of line and he could see that they could very well use him for their own purpose.**

Jesus probably knew about the Messiah stuff and knew how he and his teachings that all are safe in God who believe in Him or It or Her could be misconstrued to put him, Jesus, in the light of their expected Messiah - as one from God to make them safe; but his coming had nothing to do with becoming safe in God. He was only telling us what was true and had always been true. **We have always been safe in God, but being unaware of our true safety, we have acted otherwise - like we need God in a way different than we have Him - or Her or It - to make us safe.** He said those who were called his disciples had taken it upon themselves to install themselves in his field, but they did not belong.

It would be interesting to see how a firm traditionalist who sees Jesus only as a Messiah and not as only a wise man would interpret this verse. I am sure such a one would either dismiss Jesus offering that his disciples were out of line or would find another meaning. To each his own, but that is what I get from this verse.

Then he says that these children who are out of place will eventually have to release the field they have stolen; and when they do, all that they think they have assumed as theirs will go back to the original owners. That not only applies to his so called disciples. It applies to each one of us. **His reference to them having to take off their clothes before releasing the field is like saying that in the end, they would be left naked - without protection from the Jesus ministry because they were never part of it.**

I know this seems harsh, but I see it as realistic. Anyone can conjure him or herself as a disciple, but just claiming yourself to be one does not make you one. You have to become part of the message of the master, not just a blind follower. Traditional Christianity offers that we should accept Jesus as our personal savior blindly and trust him to save us without knowing why - or for thinking that he is needed in a different light than that in which he offered himself. It speaks to merely misunderstanding Jesus to think of him as one who is needed to save us from our sin because in reality, the sin we think we need saving from doesn't even exist - namely the supposed sin of separation of God and man.

Wanting a sin to exist does not make it exist. If I live my life wanting sin to exist and think that Jesus was a master over that unreal sin, then when I die, even though I die with the name of Jesus on my lips, Jesus will be nowhere to be found. Why? Because he represented an attitude against inherited sin, not for it. **If we die thinking we need saved from a sin we do not have, we will die in blindness and will be in effect, naked.** At least that is my take on this verse. **Naked in this verse means "unprotected."** In another verse soon to be covered, it means innocence; but here it probably means "unprotected."

But what an eye opening verse. Let him who has ears hear - as Jesus would say. The other part of this verse is merely telling us that we should live aware of the meaning of life so that we can be aware of that meaning when we pass from this life to the next. This is offered in the regular gospels too; and quite likely was taken from the Gospel of Thomas as an original source. That is merely my opinion; but it seems to me that a lot of what Thomas offers in full, the other gospels repeat in part. In other words, they took the part that was beneficial to them in treating Jesus as Messiah and left anything out that might challenge that notion. Jesus was for our becoming our own masters from insight - offered by his teachings of kindness to all because all are equally of God. It is that kindness to all that is the basis of what might be called his offered salvation - not adherence to Jesus as lord.

Verse 22:
Jesus saw children who were being suckled. He said to his disciples: These children who are being suckled are like those who enter the Kingdom. They said to Him: Shall we then, being children, enter the Kingdom? Jesus said to them: When you make the two one, and when you make the inner as the outer, and the outer as the inner and the above as

the below, and when you make the male and the female into a single one, so that the male will not be male and the female (not) be female, when you make eyes in the place of an eye, and a hand in the place of a hand, and a foot in the place of a foot, (and) an image in the place of an image, then shall you enter [the Kingdom].

Again, Jesus is offering that the true effect of salvation is having the trust of a child - of seeing things simply like a child does before he or she is thrown off course by adults who think they know better. A child left to him or herself can only learn respect for all about him or herself for what it is - a hand, an eye, a foot, a penis, a vagina. Until he or she is taught that a hand is naughty touching certain places, a hand remains a hand. Then with the notion of evil being thrown in by an adult and a warning against touching "evil places," the once innocent hand becomes a possible accomplice in a crime. This is sad. Jesus is offering that we should not confuse things like we do. We should not call "up" - Heaven - and "down" - Hell. We should not divide the world into good and evil. Up should be the sky - not Heaven; and down should be the Earth or below the Earth - not Hell. The inside of us should be the same as the outside of us. Everything and Everywhere is holy - if we only recognize that the Goodness or Presence of God is equally everywhere. **Why should the inner be**

different than the outer if the same Divine Presence is in both?

But I guess it should be obvious that those offering Heaven and Hell and dissecting reality between good and evil would not like this verse. So, when it came time for Matthew through John to copy from Thomas, they just left this one out. Oh they kept the being like a child alright, but in a different light than the intended meaning offered through Thomas. I think the others imply that being a child means being obedient to a proper authority. Since we are all supposed to obey God, that leaves the door wide open that we should obey those who claim they speak for God. To disobey is to not act like a child should. This is likely what Matthew through John believed - the need for being obedient like a child; but this verse offers a meaning that does not require authority. It offers that being a child is only lacking confusion. Right?

Verse 23:
Jesus said: I shall choose you, one out of a thousand, or two out of ten thousand, and they shall stand as a single one.

I think Jesus is saying here that in his selection process for his providence, he won't choose many, probably because many won't qualify. He will only select a few because only a few can be selected. He says he will choose one out of a thousand – or maybe only two out of ten thousand. In other words, he is implying that very few will be able to hear his words in the end. However many he can choose, though, he says, they who are chosen will stand as a single one. That is to say that in value or worth, neither of two who are chosen will be better than the other. Both will be equal because they will see themselves as equal. Two shall stand as one. That is an expression of equality.

Verse 24:
His disciples said: Show us the place where Thou art, for it is necessary for us to seek it. He said to them: Whoever has ears, let him hear. Within a man of light, there is light and he lights the whole world. When he does not shine, there is darkness.

Show us where you live, perhaps, is what the disciples were asking of Jesus. We need to go there with you and be with you. I guess that is to say that they did not know where he lived that they would ask about it; but Jesus did not answer them in terms of the place for which they were seeking. Rather, he told them that the "place" from which he came or the place at which he lived is not important. I think the irrelevance of place can be assumed because Jesus did not answer the question in terms of place. Instead he offered another evasive answer. *Show us the place where thou art* – he was asked – and he answered – *within a man of light, there is light and he lights the whole world.* What kind of an answer is that?

I think it's a Jesus kind of answer, for sure. He seemed to thrive on being mysterious and seldom answered questions in a direct manner. In this case, he was telling the disciples that it would not help them to know where he lived because there where he lived is no different than there where he was at any given moment. You think you can know more about me if you know where I live. Not so! He was saying. My light follows me wherever I go. You want to know me. Check out my light here in this place because that light is no different here than in the place where I may lay my head at night. **A man of light – or darkness – is a man of light – or darkness – wherever he is.**

I think this is good to keep in mind. It is not where we live that is important, but how we are using life. What difference does it make that I live in Laramie or Atlanta or Baghdad – as long as wherever I live, I live aware of the graciousness of life and the beauty of life and splendid of life and am grateful for it. My light will follow me wherever I go. It matters not where I live, but how I live.

Verse 25:
Jesus said: Love thy brother as thy soul, guard him as the apple of thine eye.

I think Jesus is merely emphasizing the ideal of brotherhood here. Love another as you love yourself, keeping in mind that if you do not love yourself, how can you love another like yourself?

Verse 26:
Jesus said: The mote that is in thy brother's eye thou seest, but the beam that is in thine eye, thou seest not. When thou castest the beam out of thine eye, then thou wilt see clearly to cast the mote out of thy brother's eye.

No comment needed on this one. We all know it means not to judge others because no one is in a position to know another's circumstances in life. It is best to pay attention to your own soul and get that right. Perhaps after that is done, one might be in a position to aid another.

Verse 27:
<Jesus said:> If you fast not from the world, you will not find the Kingdom; if you keep not the Sabbath as Sabbath, you will not see the Father.

I think Jesus is talking about the world of rules and regulations here - not the natural world as such. If one thinks he or she needs a lot of rules and needs to abide by a lot of law, one really does not have any sense that the Kingdom can't be bought with attention to law. Being part of the Kingdom is only having an awareness that the Living Father - as Jesus might call it - is in everyone. I think it is impossible for a person to practice a lack of compassion for everyone if one is aware that everyone has God. That awareness is what makes for membership in the Kingdom Jesus is talking about. It has nothing to do with attention to laws and regulations within society. It is law and regulation that I think Jesus would equate to "the world."

Verse 28:

Jesus said: I took my stand in the midst of the world and in flesh I appeared to them; I found them all drunk, I found none among them athirst. And my soul was afflicted for the sons of men, because they are blind in their heart and do not see that empty they have come into the world (and that) empty they seek to go out of the world again. But now they are drunk. When they have shaken off their wine, then will they repent.

I see a lesson in reincarnation here, but that is because I believe in it so much. It is my prior belief in reincarnation that I take to the table when trying to assess this verse. I think we are born into bodies as souls with the souls with which we ended our last life. It is entirely possible for souls to constantly go round and round and round without ever changing if they are the timid type who fail to take chances in life and depend on others to do for them what they should do for themselves.

Those who take chances I think might make mistakes, but they also make progress. Progress can be measured by the level of independence of spirit one achieves in a lifetime. The more dependent you are for your alleged virtue - the less progress you are making. Jesus is offering here his sorrow for so many who come into the world blind and are willing to go out of the world blind too. Jesus was offering being blind here in the sense of having to follow someone else and not know your own way around - like a blind man having to hold onto another to make his way. He said - *empty they come in and empty they go out.* Just speaks, I think, to the need of personal responsibility to get on with life and find one's own answers. In a way, it is sad, but spiritually no one can make progress for another. We can share progress we each make, but no one can actually progress for another.

Verse 29:
Jesus said: If the flesh has come into existence because of \<the\> spirit, it is a marvel; but if \<the\> spirit (has come into existence) because of the body, it is a marvel of marvels. But I marvel at how this great wealth has made its home in this poverty.

I see Jesus using gentle sarcasm here. It is like he is talking to a Jewish audience who has a sense that souls are trapped by the flesh - rather than seekers of the flesh by choosing to be born in bodies for the advantages that may offer. So many people act like their souls are enslaved by their bodies; and yet if reincarnation is a true process, it says that souls seek bodies - not the other way around.

Jesus says - if the flesh has come into existence because of the spirit, it is a marvel. I think this is a very positive statement. **Our bodies come into existence for us as souls because of the needs of our souls to live in them.** Jesus is saying that this is truly marvelous. Then the sarcasm: But if the spirit - or soul - came into existence because of the body as if the body makes the soul - or reaches out and grabs it, then that would indeed be a marvel of marvels. In other words, it can't happen. Bodies do not exist to capture souls like so many act in life like they do. **Souls seek bodies and should therefore love them when they are in them - not pretend that they are somehow captive of the body when they chose their bodies in the first place**. Jesus concludes with more sarcasm: You Jews who hate the body so - I am amazed that you choose to spend so much time in a body if it is so impoverished. In other words - if you think so little of it why does the great wealth that you think is your soul bother with such a worthless vessel? Sarcasm!

Verse 30:
Jesus said: Where there are three gods, they are gods; where there are two or one, I am with him.

I must admit I have long been intrigued by this one. Because of the great emphasis that Jesus puts on his being one with those who share his vision – as in Verse 13 – I think this one must be interpreted in that light. The emphasis should be on the last statement – not the first. ***Where there are two or one, I am with him*** could stand alone. What does he mean by that? I think he is only specifying ***two or one*** as a figurative for few – as he is specifying ***three*** as a figurative for many. In essence, he is saying that **salvation is an individual issue**, maybe worked out between two as well; however it is not a **communal issue**. It is not a matter of consensus on the part of three or more – because that will only put someone in charge other than yourself. A ***god*** could be seen as someone who **needs to control someone else**. The opposite of a ***god*** is a **solitary** – or one who depends only on himself for his virtue. If you are not a **solitary**, in effect, you are involving a ***god*** for either needing to be controlled by another or needing to control another. Where there is control, be it by you or over you, there is a ***god***.

Anyway, that is the sense of this verse, I think. If there is another besides Jesus, then there are ***two***. If there is one without a Jesus, there is ***one***. I think Jesus is only saying that if you think I am there with you and you need no other – in terms of shared vision – then I am there with you. If you have no awareness of me as a person, but are there by yourself – with my vision – then I am with you. But if there is more in your picture than you and I, then you are dealing with gods who require servitude and not virtue.

Verse 31:
Jesus said: No prophet is acceptable in his village, no physician heals those who know him.

This is right out of the regular gospels. Nothing new here. It is only to say that people do not expect to hear any kind of wisdom from those they know.

Verse 32:
Jesus said: A city being built on a high mountain (and) fortified can not fall nor can it (ever) be hidden.

I don't think Jesus is talking as much about a city fortified on a high mountain as he is suggesting that a city on top of a mountain cannot be hidden. Given other verses that offer that we should not keep our light hidden, I think this is only to offer the same kind of instruction. **Whether it is a city on top of a mountain or a lamp on top of a pole or a person sticking up for his or her principles,**

Jesus is only offering that we should not keep our testimonies hidden. Neither should we expose them on an intentional basis as in false boasting; but we should not be afraid to live our own lives and be willing to defend them in public.

Verse 33:
Jesus said: What thou shalt hear in thine ear (and) in the other ear, that preach from your housetops; for no one lights a lamp and puts it under a bushel, nor does he put it in a hidden place, but he sets it on the lampstand, so that all who come in and go out may see its light.

More of the same. **Do not hesitate to share what you enjoy**. Do not hesitate to share that in which you are proud. Put your light on a lampstand is only to say be willing to testify as to your beliefs. If you love something, take pride in sharing it.

Verse 34:
Jesus said: If a blind man leads a blind man, both of them fall into a pit.

Again, also found in the regular gospels. Nothing confusing about this one. It is to say be careful as to who you follow. If the one who leads you is ignorant or foolish, though he or she may think they have wisdom, if it is foolishness they represent and you follow their trail - both of you will share the same foolishness. Right?

Verse 35:
Jesus said: It is not possible for one to enter the house of the strong (man) and take him (or: it) by force unless he bind his hands; then will he ransack his house.

Only to say be strong in your convictions in order to withstand assaults against them.

Verse 36:
Jesus said: Take no thought from morning until evening and from evening until morning for what you shall put on.

I think Jesus was extremely soul oriented. He realized that free souls are only free to the degree that they can enjoy a comfortable independence. Don't depend too much on comforts of the world - or civilization - like clothes. Pay attention to the things that really matter. What difference does it make what you wear? **Pay attention to being grateful for life - not what you may adorn life with.**

Verse 37:
His disciples said: When wilt Thou be revealed to us and when will we see Thee? Jesus said: When you take off your clothing without being ashamed, and take your clothes and put them under your feet as the little children and tread on them, then [shall you behold] the Son of the Living (One) and you shall not fear.

I love this one. **Jesus is only offering here that I can recognize him as *"the son of the Living One"* he is only if I recognize myself as another *"son of the Living One."*** It takes one to know one. It is like that. No one can really know another unless they are like that other. That is true regardless of who it is that may be known. I cannot claim to know you and feel for what you feel unless I adopt your vision of life. Apparently, Jesus was offering that his vision of life is that it is innocent. **Nakedness reflects innocence. It says that something is good as it is.** Jesus must have believed that not only his life was good as it is, but all lives are good as they are. **He told those to whom he was talking in this verse that they could come to know him only if they imitated him.**

Many do not realize that to imitate Jesus is only to recognize one's holiness. Jesus knew he was holy - not because he had anything special the rest of us do not; but because he recognized that God is in all things. It's that being in all things that makes all things holy. One who realizes he has no sin - or separation from God - has no reason to cover up a life that is supposedly holy. Jesus suggests that one can't know him unless he can get naked without shame because when naked, Jesus was without shame. If one is without shame, it is an unconditional thing. Clothed or naked, it is all the same thing. If someone thinks he can claim to be shameless and cannot be comfortable with his or her naked being, then the sense of shamelessness is not unconditional and therefore probably not very authentic. It is pretty simple. Life is holy. Act like it. If you can't, then you can't know Jesus.

How many of those who claim to be of Jesus would be comfortable going naked to prove their innocence? First of all, most of the Jesus fans do not believe they are innocent or they would not need a savior to make them innocent - and Secondly, even under the umbrella of the innocence of Jesus, they still would not be able to claim a love of nakedness for the innocence it reflects. The test for knowing Jesus is the same now as it was then. Do you know you are innocent? If you do not, then you can't know Jesus. I do believe that most who preach Jesus today would fail that test. What do you think?

Verse 38:
Jesus said: Many times have you desired to hear these words which I say to you, and you have no other from whom to hear them. There will be days when you will seek Me (and) you will not find Me.

Only to say that we have so much time to get things right. This Jesus knew he was wise and he also knew that many of those in his audience lacked wisdom. He wanted to share his wisdom, but no one can make another wise. Each of us must listen to the wisdom of another and make it our own while we have that other available. There may come a day when that wise teacher will be gone. We need to learn when we can because delay may cause us to miss our opportunities. You know how it goes.

Verse 39:
Jesus said: The Pharisees and the Scribes have received the keys of Knowledge, they have hidden them. They did not enter, and they did not let those (enter) who wished. But you, become wise as serpents and innocent as doves.

Jesus was offering here, I think, that we should not depend on so called authorities to learn about life. In his time, the Pharisees and the Scribes were like keepers of the books in terms of the so called wisdom of life - mostly reflected in the Laws of Judaism - but Jesus is saying here that his students should not depend on the Pharisees or the Scribes, but learn wisdom on their own. Of course, their greatest teacher was Jesus himself.

The "be wise as serpents" instruction, I think, was only to emphasize that each of his students could attain wisdom on their own without dependence on anything another has to offer. Get it from within - though it helps to get it from one like Jesus too. But even if Jesus was not available, **we all have the capability of attaining wisdom on our own because it is really only a matter of good logic.**

The "be innocent as doves" instruction is only to offer that we can be innocent. **Jesus would not have told us to be innocent and find our innocence if we do not have the power to do so - again without the help of so called authorities who have nothing more to offer than what we can get from within.** We are all innocent in terms of being one with God and pure because of that. We only have to realize our innocence to really enjoy it. If we are innocent and do not know it and act like we are sinful, then we might as well be sinful because in effect, we are.

Verse 40:
Jesus said: A vine has been planted without the Father and, as it is not established, it will be pulled up by its roots and be destroyed.

I guess we all have some bad vines in our lives that we need to uproot in order to plant good vines in their place. If we are not really rooted by sound principles, eventually the bad roots we have will be uprooted and we will be left helpless.

Verse 41:
Jesus said: Whoever has in his hand, to him shall be given; and whoever does not have, from him shall be taken even the little which he has.

I think Jesus is basically offering here that it is what we have in oneself that counts. So many think that they can depend on what another has to find happiness. Jesus is telling us that salvation - if you want to call it that - is not dependent on someone else and their merits, but dependent on oneself. He says that should life end, if you have virtue in yourself, then it will only get better; but if you do not have virtue within yourself - and are maybe counting on the virtue of another - like Jesus, for instance - to save you - you will lose.

There is one important consideration about this one, though. Say that it is the end of times because of some wipe out of the Earth and its population. As long as the world continues, there is always a chance of self-improvement with a next life; but what happens if there is no next life because there are no bodies on Earth available for incarnating. In that event, all souls would be locked into what they have accomplished. If that's the case, if one is expecting another chance at life but doesn't get it, then very definitely, that which is expected will not be forthcoming and a soul would lose what it expected. In that sense, what a soul did have or expect would be taken away.

I think there is a clear possibility of this because at some point we know that some catastrophic event is going to happen - probably strictly natural - that will end all life on Earth as we know it. It has happened before and it is bound to happen again. It probably won't happen anytime soon, but who can know for sure? Just goes to argue that souls better get their act in order while they have the chance because in time, there will be no more chances - at least for some long period of time - after which maybe life will reemerge on the Earth and souls can again begin to incarnate in them. Food for thought perhaps!

Verse 42:
Jesus said: Become passers-by.

This is great advice. It is to say that we should be aware we are only passing through a life. That is not to say life is not important. **It is only to say that we should be aware that any one life is temporary.** Take heart. If any one life is filled with health problems, for instance, be aware that this life will end and maybe the next life will not be caught up with the burdens of this life. I mean, that is one way to look at it. It is important to always live life like the attitude we take with us is the attitude we will start with in the next life. Be aware that this life - or any lifetime - is temporary. Personally, I love this thought. It makes me more determined to live this life to my fullest knowing it will not last for long; and it gives me hope that whatever gains I achieve in this life can be very useful in the next.

Verse 43:

His disciples said to Him: Who art Thou that Thou should say these things to us? <Jesus said to them>: From what I say to you, you do not know who I am, but you have become as the Jews, for they love the tree, they hate its fruit and they love the fruit, they hate the tree.

Jesus is chiding anyone who thinks like the Jews he is accusing here. The Jews were of the mind that all life comes from God who is Good, but then they offered law that assumes that we are not good and need some extra grace to make us better. Jesus is not applauding that attitude that offers that a good tree can bear bad fruit. He says that is how the Jews think, but it is wrong. If the source of life is good, meaning God, then so must the fruit of God be good, meaning us.

Verse 44:

Jesus said: Whoever blasphemes against the Father, it shall be forgiven him, and whoever blasphemes against the Son, it shall be forgiven him; but whoever blasphemes against the Holy Ghost, it shall not be forgiven him, either on earth or in heaven.

I am a bit uncertain as to why Jesus would offer that blasphemy against the Father or Son is forgivable, but blasphemy against the Holy Ghost is not. I see the Holy Ghost as only being the Truth and I can understand why denial of the Truth is not forgivable because denial just leads to dead ends, but I would also think that part of the Truth is recognizing as true the Father and the Son. I do not understand how rejection of the Father and Son could not also be a denial of the Truth and therefore, unforgivable; but the important lesson here is not that denial of the Father or Son is forgivable, but that denial of the Truth is not forgivable.

I think the Father Jesus is talking about here is the source of his particular origin - his providence, as it were. The Son he is talking about here is himself as Son of his providence. I do not think he is equating Father with God or Son with God - or else there would be no question that such denial cannot be forgiven. Given he is offering that denial of Father or Son is forgivable, I think it is quite clear he can't be talking about God. Maybe that is all he is offering here. He might be emphasizing that his Father and Himself are not God; but the Truth is God. Certainly is an intriguing verse.

Verse 45:

Jesus said: They do not harvest grapes from thorns, nor do they gather figs from thistles; [for] they give no fruit. [A] good man brings forth good out of his treasure, an evil man brings forth evil things out of his evil treasure, which is in his heart, and speaks evil things. For out of the abundance of the heart he brings forth evil things.

Nothing hard about this one. It is found in the regular gospels as well. It is only to say that something good in terms of virtuous can't bear anything bad; and something bad - in terms of attitude - can't bear anything good. If we have evil thoughts or see life as evil, then we can only do evil things. If we have good thoughts and see life as good, then we can only do good things. Our hearts or our attitudes determine the worth of our expressions. It is important to make sure you always have a good heart or peaceful heart or kind heart so that you can always put forth the same.

Verse 46:

Jesus said: From Adam until John the Baptist, there is among those who are born of women none higher than John the Baptist, so that his eyes will not be broken. But I have said that whoever among you becomes as a child shall know the Kingdom, and he shall become higher than John.

John the Baptist represents someone who is very law bound. Among those who are law bound or versed and practiced in Jewish law, none are higher than John, but in the Kingdom - which we can understand as the Kingdom of Jesus - a child is higher than John. Why? Because a child has not been corrupted with law. Jesus was not praising John the Baptist here. He was offering that John and John's ways are not the way to the Kingdom. Jesus is implying that the Kingdom is only one of innocence. A child is innocent precisely because he or she has not been corrupted by law that claims to be the way to the Kingdom. Very telling indeed.

Verse 47:
Jesus said: It is impossible for a man to mount two horses and to stretch two bows, and it is impossible for a servant to serve two masters, otherwise he will honour the one and offend the other. No man drinks old wine and immediately desires to drink new wine; and they do not put new (wine into old wineskins), lest they burst, and they do not put old wine into a new wineskin, lest it spoil it. They do not sew an old patch on a new garment, because there would come a rent.

For me, this is very clear. Jesus is once again trying to tell us to ignore the old while embracing the new. The old in this case could be seen as the **Old Testament**. Sadly, very sadly, the Christian world has paid no attention to ignoring the old and has, in fact, insisted on holding onto the **Old Testament** and claiming that the new is a completion of the old. What nonsense! The **New Testament** should have pertained only to a law of love without any attention to anything in the **Old Testament. Jesus was not a fulfillment of the old. He was an initiator of the new.** I get so exasperated in this area. For me, it is so clear that we must ignore the old, not add to the old with the new. Jesus is telling us here that no one would put new wine into old wineskins; and yet that is exactly what we do by holding onto the old. Will we ever see the light? I hope so because if we don't, we will continue to rely on revelation to teach us how to live when we should just be loving one another without respect to law. Sad!

Verse 48:
Jesus said: If two make peace with each other in this one house, they shall say to the mountain: "Be moved", and it shall be moved.

What a wonderful verse! Of course, Jesus is not offering that we can literally move mountains if we have peace with one another. He is only comparing a mountain to a "problem." He is saying that if any two have peace between them, they can solve all their problems with ease. So what do we do in this world? We refuse to make peace with each other and insist that somehow we are following the counsel of Jesus in doing so. Jesus was all about refusing conflict - not insisting on it as we do. He offered that his followers should try to pass on his message of love, but if another did not want to hear it, to back off and go onto to someone who might want to hear it. Everything with Jesus was ease. He emphasized peace and the need to have it between any two. Once again, his counsel is largely ignored.

Verse 49:
Jesus said: Blessed are the solitary and elect, for you shall find the Kingdom; because you come from it, (and) you shall go there again.

For me, this is one of those verses that lead me to believe that Jesus believed in reincarnation. How can you come from a kingdom if you did not previously exist in it? To have existed in a kingdom to which you may return, you must have had a previous life. Jesus is only saying here that many in this world come from a soulful community that is Jesus like. They are of the elect only because having come from a Jesus like community, it is very likely they will return to the same when they die. I would say that many souls incarnate - both from Jesus like providences and from anti-Jesus like providences - in order to gain new members for their communities. When a soul that has incarnated for any purpose is done with his life, it is likely he or she will return to the community of origin. One is not chosen to return after being born. One is chosen - or elected - to return before being born. At least, it seems so to me. Of course it is always possible that one might not return to a providence of origin. In fact, if Jesus were to be successful, he and his kind might succeed to free some souls who came from oppressive kingdoms. That might be the very reason he came. I think so.

Verse 50:
Jesus said: If they say to you: "From where have you originated?", say to them: "We have come from the Light, where the Light has originated through itself. It [stood] and it revealed itself in their image". If they say to you: "(Who) are you?", say: "We are His sons and we are the elect of the Living Father". If they ask you: "What is the sign of your Father in you?", say to them: "It is a movement and a rest".

We are getting into more of this coming from providences again with this verse. Jesus is offering that some of his disciples probably originated from the same providence from which he came. *If they ask you from where have you originated, tell them you come from the Light where the Light originated through itself.* That is to say, they come from a place of Truth or Light and being from that place of Truth or Light, as souls of the Light, they are originating from themselves in a way. **The Light from**

the Light is only a way of offering Truthful ones from Truthful ones. The Truthful providence reveals itself through its children - Jesus and his disciples. Jesus and his disciples are the image or representatives of their providence. Jesus says that his disciples should tell the curious that they are the ***Sons of the Living Father***, but also the elect of the Living Father. We should know now what elect means. Jesus then says that if they ask you what is the sign of your Father in you - just say to them - it is a movement and a rest. **That is only to offer that coming into the world as incarnated, there is movement, but once an incarnation is complete and one returns to the providence from which he or she originates, there is rest.** I doubt that anyone else thinks that is the meaning of this one, though.

One has to guess about the use of the term *"Living Father"* when used because it seems to me that it is used to represent both God and the Providence of Jesus. In some cases, it will refer to the Providence of Jesus and in some cases, to God. One has to take note of the context of its use to know when it means God and when it means Providence of Jesus. Who knows? The original Coptic may have offered different terms when referencing the ***Living Father***, but we may be getting only one English term that in the original Coptic was several terms. Just one of the problems with trying to deal with translations.

Verse 51:

His disciples said to Him: When will the repose of the dead come about and when will the new world come? He said to them: What you expect has come, but you know it not.

What a question! *When will the new world come?* It seems we are still asking that question. Amazingly, Jesus answered it 2,000 years ago. What did he say? You have the answer above. The new world is already here. What you expect to happen in the future, Jesus said, is already happening. But it seems we did not listen when he gave the answer to our question - and we still refuse to hear the answer today. Same story. They thought the new world was to come then; and we still think it today. Sad, huh? Very importantly, however, **the new world is a "repositioning" of the dead.** We die and we are reborn. I love it because it gives me tremendous confidence that my rebirth is nothing more than a retread of my last state before my last death. Not that this verse offers that detail, but it would sure seem to be the truth. What do you think?

Verse 52:

His disciples said to Him: Twenty-four prophets spoke in Israel and they all spoke about (lit.: in) Thee. He said to them: You have dismissed the Living (One) who is before you and you have spoken about the dead.

Getting back on my soap box, once again, Jesus should not be connected to the Old Jewish Laws. He says it here again. They implied in their statement about Jesus that they saw him as one of the prophets of Judaism. What was his answer? Please, please do not include me with them. If you do, you will dismiss me for what I am trying to teach. I am not who you think I am - or should be. I am not one of your prophets. But we insisted on making him the last of the prophets. Didn't we? I get from this verse from Thomas and a lot of other verses that Jesus did not want to be connected to the old law in any way, shape, or form.

Verse 53:
His disciples said to Him: Is circumcision prof-itable or not? He said to them: If it were profit-able, their father would beget them circumcised from their mother. But the true circumcision in Spirit has become profitable in every way.

Again - we hear a refusal of the old. Jesus is not offering that at one time circumcision was useful. He plainly offers in this verse that circumcision was never useful. If he had been the expected prophet or messiah, there is no way he would have offered that circumcision was not useful. He does offer that circumcision in Spirit is useful, but that is totally disconnected from the ancient physical practice of circumcision. But again, Jesus is denying the old. How many times must he deny the old before people get the idea that - hey - he could not have been fulfillment of the old if he did not even believe in it.

Verse 54:
Jesus said: Blessed are the poor, for yours is the Kingdom of Heaven.

We get this in the regular gospels too. In my opinion, I think Jesus was offering that only the poor could satisfy the requirements of the Kingdom of Heaven, assuming here that Heaven means a kingdom of freedom. Amazingly, people do not realize that those who insist on controlling or owning things or persons in life are denying themselves freedom. The real poor do not have control over anything. It is that sense of poverty - that independence - that Jesus is applauding here. No one can be free - and therefore belong to a kingdom of freedom - if he insists on owning things - be it people or objects. **Ownership ties a person to that which is owned, thus refusing freedom to those who own.** Blessed are the poor because they have no ties to subjects and therefore are free. That is the essence of Blessed are the poor.

Verse 55:
Jesus said: Whoever does not hate his father and his mother will not be able to be a disciple to Me, and (whoever does not) hate his brethren and his sisters and (does not) take up his cross in My way will not be worthy of Me.

This verse comes right after Jesus blessing the poor. **It is only to say that if you insist on ownership of people or things, you cannot belong to the kingdom of freedom**. So many think that they must stay true to their heritage and hold onto property given them by their parents or relatives or whatever. If my father is rich and he gives me some of his riches and I use that inheritance to continue the wealth ways of my father, then naturally I cannot be a disciple to Jesus who stands for poverty and independence and freedom. **To be free in spirit, you cannot hold onto control of others.** This is pure philosophy; but who sees it as that?

Verse 56:
Whoever has known the world has found a corpse, and whoever has found a corpse, of him the world is not worthy.

This one is a bit tricky. I think what Jesus is offering is that whoever claims law or the world of law as a regimen for living the good life has found a corpse. I think Jesus would equate the world of civilized law with the "world." He is not talking about the world of Nature. He is talking about the world in regards to the society of men. Whoever believes that salvation can be achieved by attention to law without regard to the heart has found a corpse - a dead thing. The last part of this is even trickier. He is offering that the world of civilized law is not worthy of the person who recognizes that law is not the way of salvation.

Anyway, that is the gist of it. I think there is a good chance that something was lost in the translation from Coptic to English here.

Verse 57:

Jesus said: The Kingdom of the Father is like a man who had [good] seed. His enemy came by night, he sowed a weed among the good seed. The man did not permit them (the workers) to pull up the weed. He said to them: Lest perhaps you go to pull up the weed and pull up the wheat with it. For on the day of harvest the weeds will appear, they (will) pull them and burn them.

I think Jesus is offering here that it takes time for wheat to grow and mature. Comparing souls who can grow spiritually to wheat, Jesus offers that unfortunately souls who refuse to grow are planted next to souls who can grow. To harvest a field too soon would be to cut off the growing life of the wheat. So in spite of weeds (unwilling souls) living next to wheat (willing souls), the growing season should be allowed to proceed without trying to pull up the weeds before harvest time. Otherwise, the wheat could not grow to maturity. That is the gist of this one.

Who knows what the growing season amounts to? There may come a time, though, that life on this earth terminates. That could be equated with harvest time. If there is any positive message here, it is that those of us willing souls who want to do our best should not fret about the weeds that may be growing around us. Just do the best we can, I guess, and hope that the weeds don't become so numerous as to wipe us out before the expected harvest takes place. Take heart, Dear Wheat! Grow and mature and you will be harvested to join other wheat types.

Verse 58:
Jesus said: Blessed is the man who has suffered, he has found the Life.

Jesus is offering here that if you are one of those willing souls who is trying to attain what he calls *"the Life,"* persevere and you will find it - even if you have to suffer to do it. **There is certainly no value in suffering of itself, but if suffering occurs while trying to live a conviction, be encouraged.** The suffering will not last. Hold fast and persevere and you will find *"the Life."*

Verse 59:
Jesus said: Look upon the Living (One) as long as you live, lest you die and seek to see Him and be unable to see.

Nothing hard about this one. Jesus is only telling his audience to take advantage of him while he was alive because they might die without having taken advantage of their opportunities. There is a bit of a sub theme here in that once a soul has passed into its next experience and has lost the advantage of a body, it may not be able to learn. Personally, I believe this to be so. I think that souls are incarnated - or take bodies - for the advantage that a body offers. Otherwise, souls would not choose to incarnate. It would stand to reason, then, that if a soul has lived and paid no attention to Jesus while it had the chance, upon death, it would be too late. In death, we may *"be unable to see."*

Verse 60:
<They saw> a Samaritan carrying a lamb on his way to Judea. He said to his disciples: (Why does) this man (carry) the lamb with him?. They said to Him: In order that he may kill it and eat it. He said to them: As long as it is alive, he will not eat it, but (only) if he has killed it and it has become a corpse. They said: Otherwise he will not be able to do it. He said to them: You yourselves, seek a place for yourselves in Repose, lest you become a corpse and be eaten.

This one is absolutely fascinating to me. **In essence, it is saying "Get a Life" so that you will not be life for another.** My "Get a life" could be equated to his *"seek a place for yourselves in Repose."* Perhaps "repose" could be equated to "peace." If a soul is at peace with itself and with the world in general, it has found contentment and fulfillment. Contentment and fulfillment could be equated to *"the Life"* in Verse 58. I know it works that way for me. If I am contented and peaceful, it is like my life is full. Is not that finding *"the Life"*? If I am contented and peaceful, my soul has found repose.

On the other hand, if I am not contented and peaceful, then I will be unhappy and unhappy people look toward others for fulfillment. In doing that, they are subject to being eaten by those who use them. If you are not alive - as in full of life - then you are dead in comparison. You are as a corpse - and like the poor lamb who has no life left in him for being killed by others - you will become a slave to the wishes of others. The bottom line is "Get a life" of your own and find peace and contentment to avoid having to depend upon others and to be used by others for their gain - not yours.

Verse 61:

Jesus said: Two will rest on a bed: the one will die, the one will live. Salome said: Who art thou, man, and whose (son)? Thou didst take thy place upon my bench and eat from my table. Jesus said to her: I am He who is from the Same, to Me was given the things of My Father. <Salome said>: I am Thy disciple. <Jesus said to her>: Therefore I say, if he is the Same, he will be filled with light, but if he is divided, he will be filled with darkness.

I think this is basically a discussion between a lady named Salome and Jesus as to what constitutes a disciple. Salome offers that she is a disciple of Jesus - and Jesus goes off about something he calls *"the Same"* and offers that if he (one who claims he is a disciple) is really *"the Same"* or perhaps "from the Same," that he will be filled with light. **In essence, Jesus is offering that one can claim to be something all they want, but the test of their being what they claim is how they conduct themselves or how they see things.**

If I am a disciple of Jesus, the proof is seeing the truth that Jesus taught. Jesus says he is from that mysterious Same he talks about, but others could also have been from that mysterious Same. I think that mysterious Same is none other than the soulful providence of Jesus. As souls, we all originate from some soulful providence or soulful community. Many of us may well originate from a common source. When talking about that source amongst ourselves, we could say that we come from the "same" place or community of souls. But if we do come from the same community, our souls will be filled with the light of that "same" community. So the proof of anyone being a disciple - or brother - of Jesus, stemming from the "same" providence is that they would have to share a common perception or attitude with Jesus - which, of course, is love for all.

It is an intriguing thought - that we all originate from some soulful community before we incarnate in bodies on this Earth. Who knows how many of those who thought they were disciples of Jesus actually knew him for what he actually was? Salome may have been one from the "same" providence as was Jesus. From this verse, there is no actual offering that she was or wasn't. Jesus is only offering the condition of someone being a disciple of his. Did Salome qualify? We do not know. Nothing is offered about that. We only know that she thought she was qualified and Jesus was telling her what the qualifications of being a disciple of his were (and are) - that a real disciple had to share the same light or understanding about life as did (and does) Jesus. Makes sense. Right?

In that light, I doubt very much that most of the apostles were really disciples of Jesus because it seems that in general they were of Jewish persuasion that was looking for a messiah to make life right. Jesus was a person of light, as he claimed, but he was not a messiah. Any who would have concluded that Jesus was a messiah - rather than just a person of light - could not have known who Jesus was and therefore, could not have been persons of light themselves. So it seems to me.

Verse 62:
Jesus said: I tell My mysteries to those [who are worthy of my] mysteries. What thy right (hand) will do, let not thy left (hand) know what it does.

I won't get into the first part of this verse about Jesus telling his mysteries to the worthy. It might be an important idea, but the idea that engages me in this verse is the idea about not letting the left hand know what the right hand does - or vice versa. I think it amounts to not letting yourself be confused. One side of you might claim one thing and the other side do another. Jesus is only offering here that we should focus on some one thing - as in the right hand - and not let ourselves be diffused and confused with some speculation about something contrary. It is only a matter of focus that Jesus is applauding. He is not offering here any substance of focus - just that **the wise man should focus on some principle and not be sidetracked by any distractions - as from the left hand.**

In reality, this idea is not practiced well at all in the world. People will say they believe in Christ who clearly taught tolerance and love for all - even for one's enemy. Yet many Christians spout the principle with their right side and then practice something entirely different on their left side. This is what Jesus is denouncing. He is offering that we should be consistent with what we claim is right and how we act in life. **You cannot say one thing and do another. That is letting your left hand know something different than your right hand.** Be consistent. That is the message of this verse.

Verse 63:

Jesus said: There was a rich man who had much money. He said: I will use my money that I may sow and reap and plant and fill my storehouses with fruit, so that I lack nothing. This is what he thought in his heart. And that night he died. Whoever has ears, let him hear.

This one is clear. **Jesus is only offering that we should not spend our lives storing things for our physical future when we may not have a physical future.** It is pretty dumb. That is what Jesus is offering. Dumb or not, a lot of us do it. We live our lives mostly with a focus on our future within life on Earth when we should be spending our moments concentrating mostly on our spiritual present. If we do that, the future will also be secure because the future is only an extension of the present.

Verse 64:

Jesus said: A man had guest-friends, and when he had prepared the dinner, he sent his servant to invite the guest-friends. He went to the first, he said to him: "My master invites thee". He said: "I have some claims against some merchants; they will come to me in the evening; I will go and give them my orders. I pray to be excused from the dinner". He went to another, he said to him: "My master has invited thee". He said to him: "I have bought a house and they request me for a day. I will have no time". He came to another, he said to him: "My master invites thee". He said to him: "My friend is to be married and I am to arrange a dinner; I shall not be able to come. I pray to be excused from the dinner". He went to another, he said to him: "My master invites thee". He said to him: "I have bought a farm, I go to collect the rent. I shall not be able to come. I pray to be excused". The servant came, he said to his master: "Those whom thou hast invited to the dinner have excused themselves". The master said to his servant: "Go out to the roads, bring those whom thou shalt find, so that they may dine. Tradesmen and merchants [shall] not [enter] the places of my Father".

This is quite a story about some well off person inviting a lot of people to a feast and having all those he invited refuse their invitations for one reason or another. All those who refused invitations were tradesmen and merchants. So really the gist of this story is that - as is offered in the last line - tradesmen and merchants shall not attend the feast of life - so to speak - not because they were not invited, but because they were (are) too caught up with distractions to respond to their invitations. The master in this story does not exclude them from his dinner. They exclude themselves by not accepting their invitations.

And so it is with life. That is all that Jesus is saying here. **We are all invited to enjoy life - but relatively few of us accept our invitations.** Why? Because we get too caught up with storing food for the future and pay no attention to living the moment. We make excuses for not enjoying life - as in accusing it of sin - and do not accept our host's invitation to love the life we have. In essence, all are invited, but only a few accept their invitations and dare to attend to the real feast of life - which is merely to embrace life as holy and pay attention to that. Jesus emphasized the need to enjoy life now a lot in his ministry. This is just another evidence of that, I think. Jesus would not have chosen a dinner feast as the object of an invitation if he was not implying that life is a feast. So this verse tells us that life should be a feast and that we ought not refuse our invitations to enjoy ourselves and the feast of life.

Verse 65:
He said: A good man had a vineyard. He gave it to husbandmen so that they would work it and that he would receive its fruit from them. He sent his servant so that the husbandmen would give the fruit of the vineyard. They

***seized his servant, they beat him; a little lon-
ger and they would have killed him. The servant came, he told it to his master. His master
said: "Perhaps he did not know them". He
sent another servant; the husbandmen beat
him as well. Then the owner sent his son.
He said: "Perhaps they will respect my son".
Since those husbandmen knew that he was
the heir of the vineyard, they seized him, they
killed him. Whoever has ears, let him hear.***

This parable was also featured in the regular gospels of the
BIBLE – with one significant difference. In the regular
gospels, it is offered that the owner of the field will likely
destroy those who betray the host. In this version, there is
no such judgment. Why the difference? I think that the
regular gospels are intent on using the parable to threaten
punishment by the host – for disrespect of the host; but
this parable simply states what is likely to happen to someone who might be sent to disturb what has become the
status quo. Perhaps Jesus was reflecting on his own case,
realizing that he would likely be killed for challenging the
status quo. In fact, any other conclusion to his life would
have probably been unlikely – given the hard hearts of the
Jewish system and the Roman world with which he was
dealing.

I think it's good to keep in mind that Jewish Law would
have commanded that any Jew who defied Jewish Law

should be stoned to death. As I see Jesus, I see him as one proposing rule of heart only without any need whatever of attending to law. If that vision of Jesus is correct, it stands to reason that any Jew who might be seen in defiance of Law would be subject to execution according to the Law.

According to the tale of this parable, however, Jesus probably saw this Jewish system of Law as being a corruption of perhaps an intended rule of the heart system. Thus, in his tale, he offers that the rightful owners of a vineyard lose control of their vineyard to those to whom it had been entrusted. In other words, the entrusted ones defy original intent and choose to take over that with which they were entrusted without regard to the original intent of the owner – which was to reap a harvest from his grapes – which stands for liberating souls from slavery to sin.

Putting that plain, the Jewish system of harsh law was never intended. It happened, but it was not intended; and Jesus was only trying to correct the corruption that had happened by arguing for what had been intended – which is **love by rule of heart**, not **obedience by command of law.** Of what use was it to tell this tale? Some might understand it who might otherwise not understand it; however, on the flip side of that, many might misunderstand it too; and among that many are probably those who think the son was supposed to be killed as satisfaction for the very law the son actually opposed.

That is not to say, however, that Jesus as the son of this proverbial vineyard owner of this parable was sent to die.

It is only to say that – given the world to which he was sent – that would likely be his end. Notice, however, the lack of an idea of "sacrifice" in this tale. Jesus was not to be seen as a "sacrifice" to redeem anyone – as the orthodox Christians would later conclude. There is no tale of "sacrifice" here – only a tale of what would probably happen to someone who is seen as a challenge to the status quo.

Why would Jesus tell such a story? I suppose because of his awareness of his likely end. Perhaps it was to prepare any who might choose to share in his challenge to the authority of the day for what might happen to them too. In that light, Jesus may have seen himself as an example to follow in terms of being willing to do what one thinks is right without fear of death; however being willing to die for your principles for lack of fear of death is not to equate death for principle as sacrifice for others.

But many of the people who loved this verse who did not understand Jesus as merely a visionary for his providence could have sincerely jumped to the false conclusion that Jesus saw himself as the Jewish Messiah. If they had paid attention to the other verses of this Gospel of Thomas and not gone off half cocked, they would have realized that Jesus did not see himself as part of the Jewish prophets and their dismal vision of life. Thus, he could not have been a fulfillment of the wishes of prophets with which he disagreed.

But I guess enough said about that. The debate will go on about whether Jesus qualified to be a messiah or not; but, in time, that debate may change to favor a non messianic

Jesus from the previous almost universally understood and accepted messianic Jesus. When that happens, perhaps the main work that will change the debate to favor a non messianic Jesus will be the wonderful Gospel of Thomas.

Verse 66:
Jesus said: Show me the stone which the builders have rejected; it is the corner-stone.

This is in the regular gospels too. Not much doubt about its meaning. That which we reject today may become the cornerstone of our life tomorrow. **As we change in life, we see new realities tomorrow that we did not know today.** Thus, with the awareness of new realities tomorrow, we may very well embrace tomorrow what we adamantly refused today. This is still true, of course. In fact, so many of the ideas about not needing to pray to a God that is in you that we find in the Gospel of Thomas may well become the cornerstone of future thought about man's relationship with God. Knowing God is inside of me really frees me to try and appreciate that life in which He (or She or It) is. I think this is what the Gospels of Thomas and Mary are all about - realizing that we can have no sin except that which we perform out of ignorance. But it is a new version of sin; and most Christians have not put themselves to thinking about it. Thus, Thomas and Mary, as gospels, have not been considered. But tomorrow - there may be a whole different structure. I hope so.

Verse 67:
Jesus said: Whoever knows the All but fails (to know) himself lacks everything.

Anyone who claims he knows God and then proceeds to tell you all about everything outside of him or herself, while refusing to admit him or her self in his or her knowledge is one who, in practice, is not aware of the God Presence in all things. If I fail to know myself as a child of God, of what could I possibly think is worthwhile? The Jesus of Thomas was (or is) very self centered. His message was very strongly - **Know Thyself.** The reason for that is thyself is only a variant of me. If you know yourself, in ways of appreciating the blessing that is you, then you will also know me. If you do not know yourself, then how in the world could you even begin to know me - since I am, for the most part, only a version of you?

As Christ knew, you cannot really know another except by first knowing yourself; and it is how you view yourself that you will view another. Still, you must get the self right first. After that, relate to others, but first find yourself.

Verse 68:
Jesus said: Blessed are you when you are hated and persecuted; and no place will be found there where you have been persecuted.

There is no value in being persecuted on its own; but if you are persecuted because of your convictions

and you stay the course, blessed are you. That is what this verse says. Stay the course, so to speak, and once the persecution is over, you will have no awareness that it ever took place. You could have no awareness because the mind can only focus on one thing at a time. If you are focused on the blessing that is you, how could you find any time - or place - for pondering having been persecuted?

Verse 69a:
Jesus said: Blessed are those who have been persecuted in their heart; these are they who have known the Father in truth.

This is pretty much a repeat of Verse 68.

Verse 69b:
Blessed are the hungry, for the belly of him who desires will be filled.

This too, a repeat of the former Verses. Eventually your being persecuted will end and you will have plenty to eat.

Verse 70:
Jesus said: If you bring forth that within yourselves, that which you have will save you. If you do not have that within yourselves, that which you do not have within you will kill you.

Once again, Jesus is emphasizing his most treasured ideal - **Know Thyself**. You can deal with others having yourself as a base, but you cannot very well deal with yourself by having others as a base. So what happens when you no longer have others around as a base to know yourself? You will be dead, in a way. **If you go from yourself - which you will always have - to others, then you will always have a base from which to proceed.** Knowing yourself through the appraisals of others, pondering themselves, is about as useless as it gets, though. And yet many people think that they are unworthy of being known by others because they see themselves as unworthy of themselves. **If you think you need another to be completed on your own, then when that other is taken away, you have nothing.** So what happens with Paul of Tarsus when his Jesus goes away? Of course, Paul of Tarsus is counting on Jesus to always be there, but by depending on knowing Jesus to love himself, Paul is taking a huge chance that he will be lost in the great forever.

Again, know yourself first, then proceed to relating to others. Love yourself first, then proceed with that love to loving others. It works without question in that way, but it does not work from the other way around - knowing and loving self by first knowing and loving others. **The greater your independence of others for your own self awareness and self praise, the greater your self security.** This is the Jesus of Thomas in a kernel.

Verse 71:
Jesus said: I shall de[stroy this] house and no one will be able to build it [again].

What did Jesus mean by *"this house"*? My guess is that he was talking about the house of Jewish Law - if this is an accurate quote at all. He could not have been talking about anything physical because anything physical that is torn down can certainly be rebuilt. So what could he possibly have wanted to destroy? **If I know Jesus, he would be up to only one thing of destruction - and that would be to destroy false concepts.** What false concepts? Those concepts that pretend to offer that the value of man is dependent upon anything that man does.

The Jesus I know was about offering that everyone has integrity - in terms of being whole in God. All of us are holy. I think Jesus believed that. The problem is that people fail to know they are holy - or in God - because too many people go about making holiness conditional upon some extra achievement of holiness through obedience to law. The Jewish Law was all about man needing to obey some set of laws handed down through Jewish tradition to become holy. Obedience to law was required for holiness. But Jesus was aware that obedience to law cannot make anyone holy. **Holiness is a state of life that is inherited - not a state of life that can be achieved.** I think that Jesus tried very hard to offer that message in life; and it was holiness according to obedience to Jewish Law that he would have been about destroying - or the notion thereof.

Maybe at some point in the life of man, false notions about achieved holiness will be destroyed; but for now, they are as alive and well as they were in the time of Jesus. Time will tell if the future will see any kind of destruction of such outmoded ideas.

Verse 72:
[A man said] to Him: Tell my brethren to divide my father's possessions with me. He said to him: O man, who made me (a) divider? He turned to His disciples, he said to them: I am not a divider, am I?

Again, Jesus was not about law or culture. Of what did he care about how people should conduct themselves legally? The man asking Jesus was more than likely a Jew who was asking Jesus to tell his brothers to "obey the law" in terms of dividing an inheritance. Jesus could care less about such things. *Who made me a divider* - he asks? I am in no way interested or qualified to judge such things. Jesus was not about law. He was about the rule of love; and the rule of love does not concern itself with external judgments of one upon another. That is a matter of civil law - not the rule of love.

Verse 73:
Jesus said: The harvest is indeed great, but the labourers are few; but beg the Lord to send labourers into the harvest.

This one is also in the regular gospels. I guess it means that the work of salvation could use more hands. Jesus is not so much suggesting that we should ask the "lord," as it is said here for more help - as he is implying that we should pitch in and help out. He is asking us to help with his work.

Verse 74:
He said: Lord, there are many around the cistern, but nobody in the cistern.

My idea of cistern is a public bathing pool. Jesus is offering here that there are a lot of folk jostling about outside the pool - implying dirty - but none in the pool getting clean. Of course, being dirty is relative to spiritual confusion - or confusion about spiritual things. **To take a bath in this case is to rid myself of notions that prevent me from a clean look at life.** Each time I review one of the verses of the Gospel of Thomas, I am jumping into that cistern and becoming cleansed of old notions that may be keeping me from seeing life freshly.

Verse 75:
Jesus said: Many are standing at the door, but the solitary are the ones who will enter the bridal chamber.

Jesus emphasized that salvation - or the matter of salvation - is strictly a personal affair. Each one must attend to living life the best he or she can on one's own. No one should depend on another to do what is right. When an individual becomes aware of his or her own holiness, it should be like getting married. In a way, you are marrying a concept or a disposition when you become aware of your own holiness or soulful integrity within God. This marriage of the individual to a conscious active spiritual awareness of worth is the ideal we should all seek in life. It is not a "we" kind of thing. Each person must take upon him or herself the responsibility of caring for his or her own soul. It is a singular thing - not a group or social thing.

Bridal chamber is an image for happiness. People tend to think that getting married is a happiness thing. Thus, a bridal chamber can serve as an image of happiness. **Jesus is offering that it does not take two to be happy - only one.** Pretty neat, huh?

Verse 76:
Jesus said: The Kingdom of the Father is like a man, a merchant, who possessed merchandise (and) found a pearl. That merchant was

prudent. He sold the merchandise, he bought the one pearl for himself. Do you also seek for the treasure which fails not, which endures, there where no moth comes near to devour and (where) no worm destroys.

This one is found in the regular gospels too. It's meaning is quite clear. We should be not only willing, but anxious, to strive for that which we hold dear. We should be willing to sell all that we have to buy just one article of real importance in exchange. Jesus offers that we should seek for the treasure that will not fail us. What is that treasure? That which is spiritual, of course. That which is spiritual will survive this life as all in this life will eventually decay. **Our souls will not decay, however; and so we should pay attention to doing in our bodies and with our bodies what will benefit our souls because once the body is gone, the soul will not be able to benefit from the body any longer.**

For me, this is just paying attention to the idea that the body is divine (Divine). If I look at the body as divine and treat the body as divine, that translates to looking at my soul as divine and treating my soul as divine. Like Jesus says elsewhere, we should *"know what is in our sight and what is hidden from us will be revealed to us."* That is to say - as you treat your body, so also are you treating your soul. Treatment of the soul is invisible whereas treatment of the body is visible. **We can know**

how we are treating our soul which we can't see by the way we treat our body that we can see. You see, the body is only a substitute for the soul while we live in it. As we treat our body, voila, we are doing the same to our soul. We use the body to reflect treatment of the soul. At least I think so.

Verse 77:
Jesus said: I am the Light that is above them all, I am the All, the All came forth from Me, and the All attained to Me. Cleave a (piece of) wood, I am there; lift up the stone and you will find Me there.

Some consider that Jesus is referencing himself as God - or the Son of God - with this verse. He might be, but I suspect not. Putting myself in his place - or in the place of someone who may have said this - this would be my interpretation.

Anyone who sees all of existence as divine (Divine) must also see any part of existence as divine. In a very real way, for any one person who knows he or she is divine, everything should remind of that personal divinity. If I am divine and so is everything else, if I look at anything at all, I should see me in terms of something also divine like me. Lift up a rock - and there is divinity - and me. Grab a piece of wood - and you are grabbing divinity - and me. I think that is what Jesus is trying to say with this verse - though I may be wrong.

I don't think he is saying that he is special. He is only admitting to his own divinity, but by so doing, he is not denying the divinity of all. Any of us who know we are divine also know that we are equivalent to *"the All."* Everything within *"the All"* is equally divine. If we can look at anything and see *"the All,"* then, virtually speaking, we are equal to *"the All."*

I am the Light that is above them all is only to say that I am aware of my divinity and the divinity of all whereas most are not so aware. Perhaps if I have the meaning of this verse correct, I could also say that compared to most who are not aware of their divinity, **I am a light that is above them all.** Light is equivalent to vision - or seeing clearly. I see where most do not.

Verse 78:
Jesus said: Why did you come out into the desert? To see a reed shaken by the wind? And to see a man clothed in soft garments? [See, your] kings and your great ones are those who are clothed in soft [garments] and they [shall] not be able to know the truth.

More than likely, Thomas found Jesus naked in the desert. He probably did not expect that. He also found Jesus quite strong whereas he had expected to find him weak - perhaps from being in the desert with almost nothing to eat. Jesus asked Thomas - or whoever met him in the desert - *Why did you come out into the desert? To see a reed shaken by the wind? And to see a man clothed in soft garments?*

Then Jesus offered that kings and the socially elite or *"great ones"* are *those who are clothed in soft garments - and they shall not be able to know the truth* for that reason. A king or socially prominent one thinks that he or she has to dress to separate him or herself from the rest. They have to dress and dress different from the rest in order to be distinguished from the rest; but **a wise person does not need to seek distinction because a wise one does not need to see him or herself superior or inferior to others.**

Why was Jesus naked in the desert? Because it lent to the awareness he was seeking. Having done the same thing myself, I think I understand the usefulness of personal nakedness. It imprints on my soul a sense of equality; and it is equality that a soul needs in order to refuse to power over others as well as refuse to let others power over them. If I am aware of my equality, then I am not concerned at all with power. **Nakedness is the epitome of powerlessness - and holiness & equality.** That is why I go naked when I can; and I suspect that is why Jesus went naked in the desert.

In an earlier verse, one of the disciples asked Jesus when they would recognize him. He answered that *"when you take off your clothing without being ashamed."* That came in Verse 37. If he had not prefaced this Verse 78 about being without soft garments in the desert with that reference to nakedness in Verse 37, we could not be as sure that Jesus was probably comfortable with nakedness - as implied in this verse that he was found "without adornment in soft garments" - though, of course, all of this is strictly personal opinion in the end. Ultimately, each of us must make up our own mind about the usefulness of anything - be it nakedness for its imprint of holiness & equality - or about anything at all.

Verse 79:

A woman from the multitude said to Him: Blessed is the womb that bore Thee and the breasts which nourished Thee. He said to [her]: Blessed are those who have heard the word of the Father (and) have kept it in truth. For there will be days when you will say: Blessed is the womb that has not conceived and the breasts which have not suckled.

Also found in the regular gospels. **Jesus is only saying that family has no bearing on virtue.** A person offers that *"Blessed is the womb that bore thee and the breasts that nourished thee."* I suppose Jesus should have said, "Thank you," but he offered instead that blessed are those who hear the truth and attend to it.

In the end, it won't matter that Mary was the mother of Jesus. It will only matter if Mary practiced the truth that Jesus taught. Family claim on Jesus or fan claim on Jesus will not mean anything in the end. It will only matter that I heard the wisdom of Jesus and practiced it. Why? **Because virtue is its own judgment - as folly is as well.** If I practice virtue, then I will continue to practice it - in this life and after it. If I practice folly, then I will continue to do that too. It won't matter if I see Jesus or not. It will only matter if I practiced his wisdom in order to share his virtue. **Jesus cannot give me virtue. I have to earn it on my own without Jesus - and once I have earned it, it is mine.**

Verse 80:
Jesus said: Whoever has known the world has found the body, and whoever has found the body, of him the world is not worthy.

My guess is that this is a counterfeit verse, though I am only guessing. Call it an educated guess. Either Thomas did not know this verse is different than an earlier verse that offers the word "corpse" where this verse offers "body" - or someone tossed in this verse not realizing that a body is not a corpse.

Verse 56 puts it this way: *Jesus said: Whoever has known the world has found a corpse, and whoever has found a corpse, of him the world is not worthy.*

In my opinion, Verse 56 says it right. Verse 80 says it wrong. A corpse is not a body - unless it is a dead body. Verse 80 seems to be equating the "world" with the "body." I do not think Jesus intended any such equation. He intended to equate the "world of civilized law" to a corpse - a dead thing. Spiritually, law cannot insure virtue. **Virtue can only be practiced by those who know the truth, but it is knowing and practicing the truth that results in virtue - not obedience to law.**

This verse should say that one who has discovered that law is dead has found a corpse and that one who has found a corpse and knows that law is dead, of him the world is not worthy. Discovery that law is dead cannot be equated to "body" in general - only to a dead body or corpse.

Given the existence of this verse, however, that may not be authentic, it suggests that other verses may not be authentic as well. I would prefer that everything I found in Thomas (or any of the gospels) is authentic without question, but it probably isn't so. Someone other than an original gospel author may have added his or her two cents worth to some degree; and so we might get a corruption of the original Jesus as a result. That leaves it up to the discerning mind to try and separate the weed from the wheat. No one should take anything as "gospel truth" unless it appeals to his or her intelligence. The soul is far too important to let it be guided by those who have corrupted any idea of Jesus with an interpretation of their own. We all have minds. Let us use them to discern what is probably truth from falsity.

Verse 81:
Jesus said: Let him who has become rich become king, and let him who has power renounce (it).

If I have my perspective of Jesus correct, he was a fellow who did not participate in the business world of his day. Industry in terms of buying and selling just did not interest him. He says in the verse above - *Let him who has become rich become king.* I think he is only saying that those who are rich are kings, in a way. The let it happen part of the verse is really only - **let him who is rich realize he is like a king.**

And what is it like to be a king? It is to have servants. One can have servants by being either a king or one of royal order or a rich man who hires others to do his bidding. **Jesus is really saying - there is no difference between being a rich man with employees or being a king with governmental control.** In either case, **one who rules is without freedom**. One who is rich and one who rules both have others doing their bidding - but in doing so, are tied to those they rule.

After telling us that he thinks there is no difference between those who rule and those who employ, he offers that ideally, *let him who has power renounce (it).* Let those who rule and those who employ give up their claims of lordship - not so much for the benefit of those who they might be lording it over, but for their sakes - the sakes of the kings and employers. They should renounce the power they have to free themselves - as well as those they power over.

Most people fail to think this thing through - this business about being royalty with power or government official with power or business man with power. That which they fail to understand is that in being the lords they are, they are without freedom themselves. It is almost like the kings and the lords - whatever their description - are not on the high side of things with their power, but on the low side of things. Why? Because one cannot rule without being ruled by those over whom superiority is imposed. **Power corrupts the powerful by refusing them freedom.** It is one of those delicious little tidbits of which many of the rich and the powerful seem to be unaware. People who pride themselves in power are no more free than those they may subordinate to themselves.

On the other hand, those of us who are poor but are still well off enough not to be bound as servants of others are the more free. We may not have much money, but we have what money can't buy - **freedom**. The world would be so much better off if there was far more accent on freedom for all and superiority for none. Until such a world comes about, however, each of us needs to attend to our own lives and ideally choose freedom without subjugating or being subjugated - or being un-free like a lord or government official. Amazingly, freedom is only possible if you are free in relation to me. That leaves some very uncomfortable room for kings and lords. They can't attain freedom until they give up their status as employer or ruler.

Verse 82:
Jesus said: Whoever is near to me is near to the fire, and whoever is far from me is far from the Kingdom.

Not much doubt about this one. Jesus was a controversial teacher in that he tried to offer esteem without racial or national ties. In other words, he taught that each soul is independently worthy. He taught that, though, within a Jewish society that prided itself on racial or national holiness that the individual is to serve. As he would likely be criticized for his respect for the individual attitude, it only stands to reason that any who would side with him would also be criticized. If it was "hot" for him, then it had to be "hot" for any who would take up his cause.

Those who do not understand the integrity of the individual, however, are *"far from the Kingdom."* That stands to reason too. **If the "Kingdom" is a Kingdom of Individual Worth, any who would act like the Kingdom is really of social worth or racial worth or national worth first would naturally be** *"far from the Kingdom."*

Verse 83:
Jesus said: The images are manifest to man and the Light which is within them is hidden in the Image of the Light of the Father. He will manifest himself and His Image is concealed by His Light.

Jesus seemed to be one very much aware of and attuned to images. I think Jesus was very much impressed with the **"image of humanity"** in itself. It was (or is) a matter of each of us resembling or imitating our image. It is like each of us is first patterned after a blueprint. If we are smart, we will honor that blueprint first and then each of us as creations of that blueprint second. In the image of humanity, we can find the Father of Jesus because the Father of Jesus chose the image of humanity as a place of guidance for the soul. Jesus is offering that to respect the image of humanity that he and his providence chose to populate or incarnate, as it were, is to respect Jesus and his Father - or providence.

On the other hand, to smear or distrust our image - the blueprint of our creation - is also to smear or distrust all those who have chosen our image as a vehicle of trust and respect. At least, that is how I see it.

He will manifest himself and His Image is concealed by his Light is to say that Jesus and his providence are choosing the image of humanity - and humanity - as vehicles to "conceal (or reveal) their light." To honor humanity, then, is to honor or reveal the **"Light of Jesus"**; and to dishonor humanity is to dishonor or hide the **"Light of Jesus."** Rather than denigrate humanity and pretend it is somehow unholy, we should applaud humanity because it is holy. It is holy because God is within it - as God is within every image of creation chosen or not chosen by Jesus and his providence.

Verse 84:
Jesus said: When you see your likeness, you rejoice. But when you see your images which came into existence before you, (which) neither die nor are manifested, how much will you bear!

Again, Jesus is emphasizing our need to attend to our image - the blueprint of our creation. He offers that when we see our likeness, we rejoice; but when we see our images, we act like our images are "too much to bear." Jesus is being his normal sarcastic self here, I think, by stating that when we look upon our image - which is really reflected by our nakedness - we ask ourselves - how much can we bear who we are?

When you see your likeness, you rejoice is to say that we like what we wear because what we wear has become our likeness. In the process of covering up our real likeness, however, our real humanity, we are also blotting our real image. We think well of ourselves as we have chosen ourselves to be, but we think very little of the image after which we are patterned in the first place. It is not very smart to break the mirror so we do not have to look at our real selves while choosing to override our true images with socially approved conventions.

But when you see your images which came into existence before you, (which) neither die nor are manifested is to say that we pay no attention to honoring the blueprint of our creation - which blueprint itself came into existence before each of us created after it and which blueprint itself can never die nor be manifested as only a blueprint. Plans or blueprints or images cannot die. They simply are; however anything fashioned after a blueprint or plan or image can die. **As souls who occupy humanity, we are manifested, as souls, through our humanity. If we hurt humanity - or another human - we hurt ourselves as souls. If we are kind to humanity - or another human, we are kind to ourselves as souls.** Some mighty interesting thoughts passed on by Jesus that one has to dig to find.

Verse 85:

Jesus said: Adam came into existence from a great power and a great wealth, and (yet) he did not become worthy of you. For if he had been worthy, [he would] not [have tasted] death.

Jesus is only offering here, I think, that Adam lived in fear. In not knowing about life more than he did, he could not judge life or the likely consequence of it. Thus, as

everyone who does not understand life must, Adam feared
to die because of confusion about what happens after
death. Jesus said *if he had been worthy, he would not
have tasted death*. That is to say that Adam himself found
himself unworthy and because he did, he feared death. If I
think I may not find God on the other side of death, then
I may not be so willing to die as I would be if I was sure
of the presence of God. It was not so much that Adam
was found unworthy by others, but that Adam himself saw
himself as unworthy because he had a notion that it is possible to lack God.

**To see yourself as unworthy is really only to see
yourself without God**. According to the story of *Genesis*,
Adam was cast from the Garden of Eden because he suspected himself and his wife, Eve, of disobeying God. If I
see myself as disobeying God, then that automatically puts
me in some perceived opposition to God. If I perceive myself as "opposed to God" or that which is Godly, then I see
myself as unworthy of God. If I see myself as unworthy of
God, then how could I not fear death or not live in taste of
death?

But Jesus offers that Adam came from a great wealth and
power, but did not become worthy of others in his audience. That was only to say that the providence of Adam may
have considered itself very wealthy and powerful in terms
of letting Adam into the fold of humanity, so to speak, but
as smart and wealthy and powerful as Adam's providence
thought itself to be, the listeners or students of Jesus were

a lot smarter - and in that light, much more worthy than Adam who preceded them in almost total ignorance.

Jesus taught the worth of every man. So if I hear the message that I am worthy because I belong to God, so to speak, and do not oppose God like Adam felt he did, then naturally I am more worthy than Adam. I see myself as worthy; and act like I am worthy. Thus I am better off than the one who started it all - Adam - or the ones who started it all - Adam & Eve.

Why would Jesus be offering that I am better off than Adam? Because I am **without the fig leaf of ignorance** that Adam chose for himself and his wife. Many are no better than Adam, however, and still hold onto the fig leaf of ignorance that Adam chose for himself and his wife when it all began. How many still think they have betrayed God? Not only Adam, but billions of sincere souls who have lost sight of the holiness of their own image and pretend that if they cover the manifestation of their image - their own nakedness - they will find their way to God - Who or Which has somehow become disenchanted with His or Her or Its own creation. That is only seeing God in some places and not others. If I think I can find God in a creation other than my own, then I have no idea that God is Infinite and Everywhere.

Covering one's nakedness out of shame is only to betray one's real thoughts that all life itself is not holy. Doing that is to still hold onto the same fig leaf of unworthiness that Adam and Eve chose so long ago.

Verse 86:
Jesus said: [The foxes] [have] the[ir holes] and the birds have [their] nest, but the Son of Man has no place to lay his head and to rest.

Knowing Jesus like I think I do, I do not think he was complaining, though this verse sounds like he was complaining. I think Jesus chose to be a man without worldly possessions because of the simplicity of the life. He was just telling it like it was for him. Maybe there is a little complaining going on here, but he chose the life. He chose to live as a beggar and not own anything.

Why would he choose such a life? I suspect it was to demonstrate to his own soul first and then to other souls that he did not need to own anything to serve his soul. By doing so, he served as a great example for the rest of us - many of whom don't own much either. The message from it all is - if owning stuff is not important for me, then be not bothered by not owning stuff on your own. Owning things can very much tie a person down - and that can be a very sad thing.

It is really important to keep in mind that we cannot take anything with us when we die but our attitudes. All the wealth we may have enjoyed in life will be as naught then. **The wise person will prepare for the time when he or she will be stripped bare of worldly wealth and have to live on with an attitude.** If you do not own things in life, then you won't have to deal with losing things when you die. If you do not lose anything significant when you die, then you will be much more stable to continue on in the next life. Possessions can be a terrible burden. I think that is why Jesus chose to go without them.

Verse 87:
Jesus said: Wretched is the body which depends upon a body, and wretched is the soul which depends upon these two.

First things first. *Wretched is the body that depends upon a body.* What does that mean? Jesus was a champion of independence because he knew that independent souls could work out their salvation a lot easier than could dependent or interdependent souls. No one really needs another to recognize the only important truths in life. Essentially, life is divine (Divine). If we know that, be it alone or with others, then we can act in life very wisely. But often in the company of another, we can be distracted from knowing wisdom and living according to it.

If my body is dependent upon your body for its well being, then if your body is withdrawn from me, I am lost. As much as possible, we should live with our bodies as independently as possible. Every body is really the same. It is not like I should require your body to make my body well. Anything you have, I have too. So there is really no good reason for me to depend on your body for my well being.

Now for the second thought: *Wretched is the soul that depends on these two.* It is bad enough that my body should depend on your body for making my body happy, so to speak; but beyond that, if my soul has to depend upon our two bodies resolving the needs of life, then that dependency is not good. Again, as much as possible, we should try to be independent as souls so that we do not have to worry about burdensome baggage. I know it sounds crazy, but that is just the way it is.

I think Jesus was cautioning us to not lose sight of our souls, even as we gratefully invest in a body for whatever benefit that offers a soul. Wretched is the soul that loses sight of itself, however, in attending to the body. Ideally, soul and body should be as partners. Too often, souls lose sight of the **equal partnership** ideal by either accenting the body as if the soul does not exist – or accenting the soul as if the body is a useless trap. Either extreme is wrong. I think that is all that Jesus is saying here.

Verse 88:

Jesus said: The angels and the prophets will come to you and they will give you what is yours. And you, too, give to them what is in your hands, and say to yourselves: "On which day will they come and receive what is theirs?"

I guess this is to say that we all have to answer to others, even though we should live lives of solitary worth. As I see it, no one is really alone. I am not alone, though I act alone. I live in a society to which I am obligated to give my best. My best is my solitary worth, I think, but be that as it may, I still owe you and my fellow man to be the best I can be.

Now take that to what I call the **"providential"** level. If my soul comes from a community of souls (or **providence**) – like I believe it does – I am here on a mission, in a way. I am not just living for myself. I am living for my community of souls too. Thus, I will have to report to my community when I die. That is likely how it happens. My mission will be over, but it is not very likely that I will not have to account for my life to those who sent me. That is how I see the above verse.

Jesus is only reminding us that a day of reckoning is ahead for us all, but probably not before God as we think. The way that Jesus puts it – angels and prophets come to us to give us the support we need from our own kind, but eventually we will have to return to our angels and prophets to give them what is their due as well.

A prophet is normally considered to be a "spokes-man" for God; but communities of souls probably have "prophets" or "spokesmen" too. I am a "prophet" of or for my own providence; and you are a "prophet" of and for yours. I do believe in that. I have encountered in my life many of my friends who may be "prophets" of a shared providence.

I love it. I like the idea of being part of a community of souls and I love the idea that I am responsible for not only myself, but my community as well. How about you?

Verse 89:
Jesus said: Why do you wash the outside of the cup? Do you not understand that he who made the inside is also he who made the outside?

This one is a bit strange. Jesus is really saying this: **Why do you wash the outside of the cup and not the inside?** I can't imagine not washing both the inside and outside, but perhaps some do not. All that Jesus is saying here is that if we wash the outside, we should also wash the inside because both sides are made by the same creator. It is to say that we should be consistent with how we deal with life. Why treat one part of life differently than another part? Are not all parts made by the same God? It's that way.

Humans are very good for being inconsistent with life – and parts of life. We act like it is just fine to show hands and face but not the so called private parts. Why in the world is a penis more private than a hand? They are both parts; and ideally if we show one part, we should be comfortable in showing all parts. But in this day and age, we are no more comfortable with consistency of parts as were the Jews in the time of Jesus. It is not very smart to deal with our different parts in different ways. We should be consistent. That is all that Jesus is saying.

Verse 90:
Jesus said: Come to Me, for easy is My yoke and My lordship is gentle, and you shall find repose for yourselves.

Easy is My yoke he says. Note that wonderful word *easy*. **Amazingly, virtue is much easier than vice;** and yet many people choose vice over virtue. **Virtue is only treating all parts the same – as if they all have the same wonderful divine (Divine) significance.** Virtue of soul is shamelessness if the shamelessness is an expression of individual worth. How easy can it be? My life is very easy because at least I am willing to treat all of my parts alike. Society doesn't allow it in practice, but that does not matter. We are not responsible for what society does. We are only responsible for what we are in mind and intent. If my intent is to treat all of me alike, then that is my judgment.

It is so much easier to live the same ideal than to have to change practices depending on company. That is what Jesus was about – living the same ideal to the degree possible regardless of audience. That is why his yoke was so easy for him; and it is why it is so easy for me. **It is much easier to live a simple life than a complicated one; and yet many folks choose complicated over simple.** Not too smart! Such baggage comes from living complicated lives. Living a life of awareness of one's solitary worth is really all that life should be about; and it is far more pleasant and peaceful than depending on another – for their worth or their support.

Verse 91:
They said to Him: Tell us who Thou art so that we may believe in Thee. He said to them: You test the face of the sky and of the earth, and him who is before your face you have not known, and you do not know to test this moment.

I have no idea how late in the life of Jesus that Thomas jotted down this verse. It suggests, though, that the so called disciples of Jesus - or many of them - only wanted to believe, but did not, in fact, believe in Jesus. He was a mystery figure to them. When asked by the disciples that he tell about himself so that they may believe, Jesus answered that he was a bit disappointed that in spite of being with him for some time, they apparently did not know him. He suggests that a big reason for their not knowing him was because they failed to **"test"** him. I believe this really means they failed to **"imitate"** him. The word "test" may a bit misleading. If it were me talking to a bunch of guys who I think failed to know who I am, I would know immediately that they did not know me because they did not imitate me. **Imitation is the surest form of understanding**. That is doing what I do - not just as a blind copy cat, but as a person of understanding doing what I do because you believe as I.

I may be wrong, but I suspect that it was clear to Jesus that they failed to understand him because clearly they failed to repeat his conduct. Maybe some of that conduct was shameless nakedness. There is ample suggestion in the Gospel of Thomas that Jesus believed in shameless nakedness. See Verse 37. If he went naked, but others around him did not, then it would have been clear to Jesus that they did not know him. The details of their failure is not clear, but it is my guess that they showed misunderstanding by failing to imitate Jesus. **This is sad because these same poor students would later go forward offering Jesus to the world but offering a false Jesus - not because they were insincere, but because they just plain did not know the man they claimed to know.**

Verse 92:
Jesus said: Seek and you will find, but those things which you asked me in those days, I did not tell you then; now I desire to tell them, but you do not inquire after them.

This suggests that Jesus measured what he tried to teach according to some standard - that standard being an impression on his part that his students were capable of understanding. He said that they asked questions before this time - probably late in his life - but he did not answer them. He did not answer them because he did not think they were ready for his answers. Perhaps he was waiting for some manifestation of his disciples understanding some earlier teaching - including example - before answering their questions. But apparently they grew tired of asking - probably because they failed to grasp his general message of the intrinsic worth of all beings. Still he was anxious for them to learn and he was hoping they would repeat earlier questions, but they never knew enough about the man to even know the questions they should ask - even though they had asked them before.

This lack of understanding must have been very frustrating for Jesus. His disciples apparently were impressed enough to know he stood for something, but it seems they never learned just who he was or what he actually believed.

Verse 93:
<Jesus said:> Give not what is holy to the dogs, lest they cast it on the dung-heap. Throw not the pearls to the swine, lest they make it [   ]. **(These brackets around an empty expression imply, I think, that the translators could not make out what came here. Rather than guess, they just left it open. But there is enough they could translate to make some sense out of the verse.)**

It may seem like Jesus is talking about some other than his disciples, but given earlier verses offering that his disciples did not know him, this verse could just as well be directed to his disciples as to any strangers. I know it has happened to me. I have had some wonderful notion to share, but to try and share it with others who have no good impression of me is like to throw myself or my ideas *to the dogs*. But Jesus was also talking in generalities here. It is good advice. **Don't waste your time trying to offer wisdom to those who have no interest in wisdom.** One has to be open to wisdom to understand it. It was true in the days of Jesus - and it is still true today.

Verse 94:
Jesus [said]: Whoever seeks will find [and whoever knocks], it will be opened to him.

It is true. Anyone who truly seeks will probably find; and if you knock, a door will open for you. But you have to be a genuine seeker to find and you must knock on the door of a wise person to have him or her open his or her door to you. Pretty simple stuff. This is to say - be active and not passive about learning. Get after it. Don't expect someone to come to you. You must have the initiative to go to one with the answers and not expect things to just drop into your lap.

Verse 95:
[Jesus said]: If you have money, do not lend at interest, but give [them] to him from whom you will not receive them (back).

This is only to say that we should be interested in help-ing others for their sakes and not do what we do in order to get back something. Getting interest from a loan is to loan for the sake of profiting from your loan. **To loan and only expect back what you lent and nothing more is the ideal. If possible, of course, it should even be more than that. When we can, we should not even loan, but give away - expecting nothing in return, not even the money or value lent.**

Verse 96:
Jesus [said]: The Kingdom of the Father is like [a] woman, (who) has taken a little leav-en [(and) has hidden] it in dough (and) has made large loaves of it. Whoever has ears, let him hear.

Jesus is only saying here, I think, that what Jesus is call-ing the ***"Kingdom of the Father"*** is like a little idea that makes for a huge impact. To look at a big loaf of bread, one would never guess that it is big only because of a "little leaven" or yeast that has been added. What is the "little idea" that has a huge impact? My guess is that it is the idea that God is everywhere - or as Jesus expressed in Verse 3, ***the Kingdom is within you and without you.*** That is to say the same thing that the Kingdom is everywhere. Once one comes to realize this little truth, entire lives can be changed. That little idea can have a huge impact.

What is the ***Kingdom of the Father?*** In this case, I think it only means **"God's Kingdom."** God's Kingdom is literally "infinite" embracing all things and all existence. **It is not a moral truth so much as a real truth.** One can realize a moral imperative from the idea, but essentially it is only a statement of fact - God exists everywhere - within us and without us - or outside of us.

Verse 97:

Jesus said: The Kingdom of the [Father] is like a woman who was carrying a jar full of meal. While she was walking [on a] distant road, the handle of the jar broke. The meal streamed out behind her on the road. She did not know (it), she had noticed no accident. After she came into her house, she put the jar down, she found it empty.

This is to say, I think, that the ***Kingdom of the Father*** (or God) does not depend on the intentions of man. I am not sure why he made the comparison, but Jesus offered that a woman carrying a jar of meal was totally unaware that the meal she was carrying had spilled out of the jar. That meal spilled without her being aware of it; and the spilling is being compared to the ***Kingdom of the Father.*** That is to say, I think, that Heaven does not depend on us.

Too often, I think, mankind thinks that Heaven depends on it to happen – as if God is dependent on man to achieve His or Her or Its Presence. Jesus is only saying here – though very awkwardly, I think, that Heaven (or the **Kingdom of the Father**) is happening in spite of mankind's intention or awareness. The important notion to get from this, though, is that Heaven does not depend on us. It happens because the **Kingdom of the Father** is within us and without us. In no way, does it depend on us. That is all this verse intends to say, I think.

Verse 98:
Jesus said: The Kingdom of the Father is like a man who wishes to kill a powerful man. He drew the sword in his house, he stuck it into the wall, in order to know whether his hand could carry through; then he slew the powerful (man).

Though the **Kingdom of the Father** does not depend on us, our realization of it for ourselves does. If we are wise, we will know what we are about so that we can better realize our purpose. Jesus is only offering here that it is smart to test ourselves with our weapons before we set forth to use them. He is only suggesting that it is foolish to face an enemy without first having tested the weapons we might want to use against him.

We should practice our skills to know if they will be enough to do what we want to do. Jesus is not suggesting that any one should slay another with this verse. He is only saying that if one were to want to kill another, he should test himself for the task beforehand in order to assure success. The key here is "test." If it is desired to kill a man with a sword, then make sure the sword has a sharp enough point on it to penetrate an alleged enemy. **Plan what we do, but test what we plan.**

How would this apply to the spiritual life? My guess is that any worthwhile objective of the spiritual life is peace. Peace is merely being at ease. If what we are doing with our minds and souls is not making us peaceful, then we should know that what we are doing is not producing peace. All we have to do is test any notion we have. Does it produce peace? Yes – then we can be confident that our plan for life is working. If the answer is No – then we can be confident as well that our plan for life is not working. If it is not working, then we should try another sword, another way. Test that. And so forth.

Verse 99:
The disciples said to Him: Thy brethren and Thy mother are standing outside. He said to them: Those here who do the will of My Father, they are My brethren and My mother; these are they who shall enter the Kingdom of My Father.

He says only those who *do the will of My Father* can enter his kingdom or community of souls. Who are those? Virtually speaking, all of those who treat everyone equally, knowing that all are *sons of the Living Father.* That would be my guess. If the human family of Jesus did not respect that principle, then they would be excluded from membership because membership is tied to character of a life lived, not to a blood line or national or racial affiliation. It makes sense. Right? In essence, the Kingdom of Jesus is one of Peace**; but peace is derived from being content with one's equality within the entire Creation of God, not assuming inequality based on alleged diverse origin or merit.**

No matter how you may treat me, to do the will of the Father of Jesus – or Jesus himself – I must treat you with kindness due to your equality of divinity (Divinity) as being an equal *son of the Living Father.* If I treat you badly because you have treated me badly, then your character of inequality becomes my own; and once that happens, I have lost peace; and if peace is lost, so also is membership in a kingdom of peace.

Verse 100:
They showed Jesus a gold (coin) and said to Him: Caesar's men ask taxes from us. He said to them: Give the things of Caesar to Caesar, give the things of God to God and give Me what is Mine.

Jesus is only saying here that giving depends on the recipient. If I have a dollar in my hand and give it to God, then my gift is rather useless. God does not receive dollars because God is not about dollars. If I have a dollar in my hands and give it to Jesus, then he might tell me it is of no use to him. If I have a dollar in my hands and give it to you or the government, then, fine, it is useful. Jesus is only saying that we can't give except as according to the needs or character of the receiver.

He says that we should give to God the things that are God's. What is that? I would say that is only **awareness that all life comes from God and gratitude for that gift.**

Jesus said to give him what is his and by so doing offered a distinction between him and God. Give to God what is God's and give him what is his. So what is his that is not God's? What would personally belong to Jesus? I'd say respect for his providence which stands for peace due to the equality of the divinity (Divinity) of all. I really doubt he would want anything else. Just respect for that which he stood. And what did he stand for? **The dignity of the individual due to his or her divinity.** If I had to come up with an answer, that would be it. He came to teach us of our dignity. So by believing in the dignity he taught, we would be giving him what he deserves.

All Jesus wanted us to be aware of is that - according to Verse 3 – we are ***sons of the Living Father.*** That is not just some of us. That is all of us. I can only give to Jesus what he deserves by believing his teachings and conducting my life accordingly. Anything less would be disrespect; and that is certainly not something that he deserves. Is it?

Verse 101:

<*Jesus said*>: *Whoever does not hate his father and his mother in My way will not be able to be a [disciple] to me. And whoever does [not] love [his father] and his mother in My way will not be able to be a [disciple] to me, for My mother [   ] but [My] true [Mother] gave me the Life.*

Getting close to the end of the gospel, the final entries were perhaps a bit more tattered than the earlier verses. The translators did the best they could, I guess, but where there are brackets without contents, they could not make out Coptic words. My translation is one of the earliest - 1959 - and the translators were at least honest in not offering their own expectations where original words were blurred - probably due to the age of the manuscripts. Let's face it. The Coptic work of the Gospel of Thomas had been in a cave for over 1600 years - without anyone knowing of its existence. Thanks to some conscientious monk or whatever, when the powers that be in the 4th Century directed that certain works like the Gospel of Thomas be destroyed, that fine monk (or monks) did not obey and hid the banned works in a cave off the Nile River in Egypt. There that work - among others - stayed hidden until 1945 when a peasant accidentally stumbled upon it. But age certainly had to have had some impact, causing some erosion of words.

Be that as it may, this verse is also found in the regular gospels. It only offers that to be a disciple of Jesus, the counsel of Jesus must be respected. If I claim to be a disciple of Jesus, and follow instead the counsel of a parent, then obviously, there has to be a conflict. Who knows what Coptic word was found where the translators placed the word "hate"? Of course, it should not be taken literally. Jesus is not saying we should hate our parents if they teach other than he does. He is only saying that we can't be his followers if we respect any conflicting opinion over his own.

Commenting on the last part of the verse, *for My mother [   ] but [My] true [Mother] gave me the Life,* the translation is unclear, though the meaning, I think, is very clear. **Jesus is offering that his true parents are those who bore him his soul, not his earthly parents who gave him his earthly body.** He is only offering that we need to be aware - like he is - that our true Mother or Parent - of the soul - is the parent we must respect the most. Dad and Mom are only like us, of the same earthly heritage, but our souls are children of a much more important parent - our soulful parent. Some would take this to mean God. Personally, I do not. I think my soul comes from another soul originally just like my body came from another body. I think Jesus had that same sense of soulful parentage; though I suspect that none of his disciples understood his belief - perhaps including Thomas. But that is only my opinion - just like all of my comments are.

Perhaps the reference to his soulful parent as "Mother" rather than "Father" is of some relevance here. Mother would be a more fitting term to use than father for Jesus when talking about the origin of his soul because he would have wanted to offer a clear distinction between God - Our Infinite Father - and his parent soul - his mother. My mother gave me life, he says - or at least, the translator saw the expression "mother" here to be the intent.

It fits for me because personally I distinguish between my parent soul and the God of all souls and all bodies. People who are unaware that their souls came from other souls and not God are apt to misinterpret a lot about life. When we see God as our personal parent and do not recognize what might be called an evolutionary parent, then our confusion is apt to lead us into all sort of confusion. We make God responsible for this or that about us when it is not God Who is responsible - but our various evolutionary parent or parents - be they of the body or the soul. But that is a discussion that belongs to a different venue.

Let me comment here that in the '80s, I wrote an essay type work I called *UNMASKING THE SOUL*. Recently, I included that work in a printed work or book I called *EXPLORING THE SOUL - AND BROTHER JESUS*. See the end of this work for a reference to that book as well as to other books I have published; but in that book I call *EXPLORING THE SOUL - AND BROTHER JESUS*, I analyze the soul and its likely origin and destiny - as well as Jesus, repeating a lot there that is included here in this interpretation of **The Gospel of Thomas** - and later - **The Gospel of Mary Magdalene**. If interested, feel welcome to check out my work on the soul and Jesus - as well as any of my other books. OK?

Verse 102:

Jesus said: Woe to them, the Pharisees, for they are like a dog sleeping in the manger of oxen, for neither does he eat, nor does he allow the oxen to eat.

Jesus is offering that woe should belong to those who are arrogant like the Pharisees. Perhaps being responsible for safeguarding the scriptures, they really did not pay much attention to the scriptures for their own sakes - and neither did they allow others to read the scriptures. I don't think any more needs to be said about this verse. It does not really say much in terms of offering wisdom. It merely comments on what Jesus saw as arrogance and clearly repudiates that kind of conduct as woeful.

Verse 103:

Jesus said: Blessed is the man who knows i[n which] part (of the night) the robbers will come in, so that he will rise and collect his [   ] and gird up his loins before they come in.

Also found in the regular gospels. It is only to say that we need to live our lives ready to die at anytime.

Verse 104:
They said [to Him]: Come and let us pray today and let us fast. Jesus said: Which then is the sin that I have committed, or in what have I been vanquished? But when the bridegroom comes out of the bridal chamber, then let them fast and let them pray.

In an earlier verse - Verse 14 - in part, Jesus said: *If you fast, you will beget sin for yourselves, and if you pray, you will be condemned.* That is because, I think, that the only ones who think they need to fast and pray are those who think they need to appeal to a God outside of them. For what other reason would you need to fast and pray? So, fasting and praying, expecting some reward from God for doing so, is useless. **If God is already inside of you, of what need is there to pray and fast as if God is not inside of you?**

Given the earlier warning about the uselessness of praying and fasting (to impress God), Jesus is not suggesting prayer and fasting here - as it might be implied. He is only offering that if it were so that there is no bridegroom about, then praying and fasting might be useful. In fact, however, Jesus was about and is about. He was married to the truth as we should all be married to the truth. That is what Jesus means by bridegroom here, I think - one married to the truth and happily secure because of it. The condition of fasting and praying, then, becomes un-fulfill-able - as it were - and thus prayer and fasting (to impress God) is never of any use.

Verse 105:
Jesus said: Whoever knows father and mother shall be called the son of a harlot.

Jesus is only, once again, citing the importance of our not following the advice of anyone - including our evolutionary parents - if we choose them over Jesus. Given his earlier warning about needing to "hate" father and mother if their counsel is not the same as his, we can be sure he is only continuing that warning here. Of what good is it to anyone to adhere to the advice of their evolutionary parents if that advice is a path to perdition?

Upon further reflection, my impression of harlot is a whore or one who is a prostitute or one who is willing to sell him or herself for a price. Makes sense that being caught up with having to sell yourself for a price while becoming oblivious to wisdom would not be good for the soul. All Jesus is saying here is that life is precious and we ought to be about living it wisely - not fretting our lives away being prostitutes and losing sight of the real treasure of our souls.

Verse 106:
Jesus said: When you make the two one, you shall become sons of Man, and when you say: "Mountain, be moved", it will be moved.

Knowing Jesus as I think I do now, since Jesus referred to himself as **"Son of Man,"** he is saying here that we can become like him and realize we are respectable *"sons of Man"* if we do what he does - see everyone as equally children of God. ***When you make the two one*** is a way of offering that we should not be caught up with our differences, but be impressed with how we are alike. If I see you as I see myself, then only peace results. It is when we insist on "being different" that we engage conflict in life and lose peace. **If we see ourselves as equal children of God and act like it, there is no problem too big to be solved.** That is what he means when he says that if we make two one, we will be able to move mountains. A mountain is only a symbol for a "big problem." If we are impressed with our equality and not our differences, we can "move mountains" or solve any problem we may encounter.

Verse 107:
Jesus said: The Kingdom is like a shepherd who had a hundred sheep. One of them went astray, which was the largest. He left behind ninety-nine, he sought for the one until he found it. Having tired himself out, he said to the sheep: I love thee more than ninety-nine.

This one is certainly confusing. I think it is the source of the parable of the lost sheep as offered in the regular gospels, but in the regular gospels, the lost sheep is not referred

to as "the largest sheep." In the regular gospels, the impli-
cation is that every sheep is important and that if one gets
lost, the Father of the Kingdom will pursue that lost sheep
as if it is the most important one of all. He would even be
willing to leave the others who have not strayed and go
after the lost sheep. It is comforting to think this, but I do
not believe that is what Jesus is saying here.

Why would the sheep that is the largest be the one that
strays? It is not just any of the sheep that strays, but the
largest one - the one you would think is the least vulner-
able. Because it is the largest sheep that goes astray, I think
this is to refer to the largest sheep as Jesus himself. I think
that the other sheep should have strayed with the largest
sheep, Jesus, but perhaps to stay seemingly safe, they let
Jesus go out by himself. But Jesus will not be allowed to
go by himself. The Father of the Kingdom of which he is a
part will go after him and not let him be alone. The other
sheep should have followed Jesus, but did not.

The 99 who did not stray and "follow their leader" are
part of the overall gang of souls sent to do the mission
Jesus. It should not have happened that way. Perhaps the
99 are the so called "disciples" of Jesus who should know
better than to huddle in safety and, in a way, betray the
mission. What was the mission of Jesus and his disciples?
To spread the good news of the kingdom. And what was
the good news of the kingdom? The previous verse tells
all. ***When you make the two one***, that is the key to belonging to the kingdom (of peace). But as history has

shown, the disciples did not make the two one and favor equality among beings. In other words, the disciples who should have been about the same equality ministry that Jesus came to promote chose to stress inequality - or that Jews were the chosen ones of God. Jesus came to disagree that any of us can be chosen over others, but the regular disciples stayed with the "chosen race" nonsense of Jewish tradition. **In essence, they abandoned the plan.**

Well, anyway, that is how I see it. Jesus was not alone from his providence. Lots of souls came with him, but for some reason, they became lost in the game of inequality and did not stay true to the mission. The 99 sheep are fellow sheep of Jesus, from the same providence or soulful community, incarnated among humans to show incarnated souls the way of equality. *When you make the two one -* says it all. Do not insist on inequality or treating others like they are unequal to you. Why? Because if you do, peace will be lost. It is as simple as that. **Sadly, the lesson of Jesus and the lesson of equality was greatly lost because the "disciples" of Jesus lost their way.** Too bad!

At the end of the parable, the Father tells the lost sheep - *I love you more than the ninety-nine.* Why would he say that? Because Jesus is a favored one of the 100 sheep. **As the "main one," on this collective mission, it would naturally follow that he would be loved more than the others - in a way.** Jesus was certainly for equality, but even among equal ones, souls choose favorites. Some might think that favoritism is a violation of the principle of equality; but think about it. I can spend a lot more time with one person than another in life, but having compared them equally in terms of being equally children of God, I would still choose my companion over the stranger. **When the Father says he loves Jesus more than the others, it is simply favoritism due to established companionship more than anything else.** At least, I think so.

Verse 108:
Jesus said: Whoever drinks from My mouth shall become as I am and I myself will become he, and the hidden things shall be revealed to him.

Whoever drinks from my mouth and adopts the principle of equality *shall become as I am.* And what will happen if I should become like Jesus and embrace equality? **Hidden things shall be revealed to me.** What is hidden? For one, the cause of conflict. Strangely, it is only by actually treating others as my equal that I can see the truth. What is the truth? **Inequality divides and causes conflict as equality unifies and makes for peace.** It is easy to see that as a truth if you live by the principle that equality is the basis of peace.

People get lost when they become confused. Confusion happens when equality of being is abandoned. When people live their lives making two individuals totally separate and emphasizing the difference between them rather than the unity of them, then hidden things are also kept hidden and confusion continues. If you insist on confusing things, not only will you not be able to move mountains, you will not even be able to move hills. **Confusion and inequality disables. Equality - or making the two, one - enables.** But you have to live the life to see it. All the argument in the world will not let you see the truth unless you first live it.

Verse 109:
Jesus said: The Kingdom is like a man who had a treasure [hidden] in his field, without knowing it. And [after] he died, he left it to his [son. The] son did not know (about it), he accepted that field, he sold [it]. And he who bought it, he went, while he was plowing [he found] the treasure. He began to lend money to whomever he wished.

This is to say, I think, that not all is lost if an idea is not at first embraced. The hidden treasure that is buried in the field is like the truths of Jesus. Those truths are handed down through the generations with the various generations being unaware of the treasure of them. For example, people keep passing along the parables of Jesus without understanding what they mean. Eventually, however, someone is going to buy the field that contains the treasure of equality - or the principle of equality - or making two one - and he will prosper unlike all those who proceeded him with the field with the treasure in it. Eventually, then, the truth will be discovered and the meaning of the parables will be known. When that happens, the one who finds the treasure and discovers the hidden truth (or truths) of the parables will be able to share his or her wealth at will with whomever he or she meets.

Verse 110:
Jesus said: Whoever has found the world and become rich, let him deny the world.

This is only to say that if you are among those who insist on living in the world of inequality and have become worldly rich as a result of it, it would behoove you to know that true wealth of soul is about "denying the world" of worldly riches - not embracing inequality and worldly profit at the expense of spiritual profit. Jesus is only telling it like it is. If you are into inequality and insist on living according to that principle, you may become rich in this world alright, but perhaps at the cost of your very own soul.

Verse 111:
Jesus said: The heavens will be rolled up and the earth in your presence, and he who lives on the Living (One) shall see neither death nor <fear>, because Jesus says: Whoever finds himself, of him the world is not worthy.

Sorry! These last verses were difficult for **Mr. A. Guillaumont** and his team of translators to translate - from Egyptian Coptic to English. My translation is one of the earliest - 1959 - and my translators were honest enough not to act like they knew every word. Age blurred some words. I have read many translations that simply offer verse like there never was any complications or blurred words. I am mighty grateful that my copy is one of the earliest and has the integrity to admit confusion where age blurred the original Coptic.

So, to get on with the translation of this verse, I think it offers that at some point, life on Earth will end. ***The heavens will be rolled up and the earth in your presence,*** I think, says that life, as such, on the Earth will end. It is hard for me to imagine that someone in the time of Jesus could have known of the future like seems to be established in this verse. Was Jesus aware of the Cosmos? It seems that he was because I think he was aware that at some time something would happen - possibly, cosmic wise - that would declare an end to life on Earth.

I think the Jews of the time looked at heaven as being "in the skies." I think that Jesus was offering here that those skies would end in terms of being available for some mystical kind of ascent. Why? Because there would be no life on Earth to look to them anymore.

Just speculating off hand, there are probably many things that can cause an end to life on Earth. Maybe some celestial body will crash into the Earth and completely wipe out all life. Who knows? Life on Earth has probably ended many times due to some cosmic event that may have caused an instant ice age or some calamitous end of life on Earth.

Personally, I do not fear man upending the Earth, though it is definitely within the realm of possibility. Maybe Earthlings will end life by themselves via some catastrophic world wide war. I doubt it, but it could happen I guess. If that happened, then, yes, it might have been due to human activity or human insanity or human madness, but that is pure speculation. It is worthwhile to ponder, but in the way I am talking about the end of the Earth, it does not matter one iota how it ends. It just matters that at some point, it will end.

And when it ends, what will souls without bodies do? Up to the end of the Earth and its generation of life, there would have been bodies galore available to incarnate, but what happens when there are no more bodies? Interesting speculation, but **my guess is that souls would be "frozen" in whatever state they were in when incarnated life ended.** There would be no more chances to reincarnate and try to change a soul. As a soul would be found at the termination of life on Earth is how it would remain - perhaps for millions of years - at which time, maybe a new spring would come about and new life on Earth could emerge and new incarnations could proceed.

But what does this say about the need for each of us to get it right? Well, if you don't think that being "frozen" in some less-than-ideal state is worth trying to find peace in this life before there is no more chance for change, then you may be among those who will be frozen in a less-than-ideal state. I won't go into those possibilities. **Suffice it to say, that if my state is not a state of peace at the time of a final interruption of life, reason would say I may drift a long time without benefit of peace.** Now, is that anyway to spend an eternity?

On the other hand, if life on Earth did end, who is to say that souls that would have incarnated on the Earth can't locate to other worlds - even other galaxies? My guess is that such would be possible - and maybe even probable. Even if life on Earth does not end, maybe souls can choose to locate to other Earths or other creations, so to speak. Who knows? Personally, I think it is likely that planets like our Earth are repeated often elsewhere in the **Grand Universe of Existence**, in general. Given that "probability," when any of us die who lived on Earth, we may simply locate to another Earth somewhere else; but if so, wherever we might go, we would still have to inherit the same "earthly soul" we may have thought we were leaving behind. It is certainly an intriguing thought. Isn't it?

The last part of Verse 111 is a repeat of other verses. Jesus was emphatic about not being caught "with the world." *Whoever finds himself, of him the world is not worthy* is a way of offering that "the world" is high on having no knowledge of self. Jesus was very strong on the idea that self awareness and self esteem is the key to peace. The world often teaches that we must sacrifice the individual for the sake of the lot. Jesus would not agree. In Verse 3, Jesus said, ***the Kingdom is within you and without you. If you will know yourselves, then you will be known and you will know that you are sons of the Living Father. But if you do not know yourselves, then you are in poverty and you are poverty.***

Jesus was all about our "knowing ourselves" because if we have such knowledge, we will also be aware that we are ***"sons of the Living Father."*** If I do not know I am a son of the Living Father, then I do not know myself. Jesus emphasized the importance of self awareness, knowing that each of us is a ***"son of the Living Father,"*** but if we are unaware of our status, then we might as well be the son of whoever it is we think gave us birth - like Satan for instance. **If we do not know who we are, then we are indeed in poverty and are poverty itself.**

Whoever finds himself - and knows he is truly a son of the Living Father - or God - of him the world is not worthy. Given that "the world" stands for civilization that does not consider the integrity of the individual as important, Jesus is asking us to stay clear of such a world. That world is not worthy of us because it is not even worthy of itself. Well, the meaning is clear if we want to look for it.

Verse 112:
Jesus said: Woe to the flesh which depends upon the soul; woe to the soul which depends upon the flesh.

We are born to find self-esteem and we are borne into bodies that help us to do that; but we should always be aware that at some point in time, ***"the heavens will be rolled up and the earth in your presence."*** At such time, there will be no more bodies to incarnate - at least for some eons of time - barring that there is not "another Earth" someplace else - which I do believe there probably is. Be that as it may, the wise soul will realize that it has to go on by itself and will not live life dependent on a body. **We should cherish our bodies, sure, because they are the very vehicles by which we can learn self-esteem, but to act like we are only bodies that die in time and that we never survive as souls alone is not smart.** Is it?

Jesus is only offering here that the wise person is aware of the **"facts of life and death."** Life will end for the body - both temporarily and at some point, virtually permanently - and only the soul will continue in whatever state it left the world. We should love our bodies because they are our vehicles of salvation, in a way, but we should always be aware that our souls exist independent of them.

Verse 113:

His disciples said to Him: When will the Kingdom come? <Jesus said>: It will not come by expectation; they will not say: "See, here", or: "See, there". But the Kingdom of the Father is spread upon the earth and men do not see it.

If this thought does not open your mouth in awe, nothing can. It says everything. How many times have we been told that so and so is inspired of God and is offering that he or she can "lead us to Heaven." Nonsense! That is what Jesus is saying. Do not believe anyone who comes to you - in his name or otherwise - and offers that Heaven is someplace else. He is saying, it is right here and right now. *"The Kingdom of the Father is spread upon the earth and men do not see it."* Heaven is already here - or anything we might want to be Heaven.

Can there be a "better Earth" someplace else? Not if God is everywhere. Jesus is offering us here that God is everywhere. The Kingdom (of God) is everywhere. It has nothing to do with place. It only has to do with a state of mind. If I have Heaven here, no matter where I go in a next life, it will follow me - or I will follow it. **Whether it is in a body or outside a body, as long as I am aware that I am truly - like you and everyone - a** *son of the Living Father,* **then I have found a perfect state.**

145

Verse 114:
Simon Peter said to them: Let Mary go out from among us, because women are not worthy of the Life. Jesus said: See, I shall lead her, so that I will make her male, that she too may become a living spirit, resembling you males. For every woman who makes herself male will enter the Kingdom of Heaven.

What a way to end it! The Jesus of Thomas emphasizes equality. He is continuing to do that here. In Verse 106, Jesus said: *When you make the two one, you shall become sons of Man, and when you say, "Mountain, be moved", it will be moved.* **When you make the two one. That is the key.** When you see yourself as equal to me and me equal to you. When there is no longer a variance of quality between us because there is an equality of esteem between us and within us, then we can move mountains - which figuratively means, "solve huge problems."

But what have we done? In the very name of the man who forbid it for the sake of peace, we have insisted on keeping two as two. We have not paid any attention to being one. We have insisted that there is good and evil, not just good. We have insisted on two when there should be only one. We have insisted on distinguishing between two and have named one an infidel and the other a faithful one. We have insisted on separation. We have insisted on division; and we have been plagued with it.

What is the current war in Iraq but an insistence on making two, two? Us against them, them against us! It is all wrong for the sake of individual peace; and it could never lead to universal peace.

In the times of Jesus, the female was considered less worthy than the male. It is even admitted here. Peter says *Let Mary go out from among us, because women are not worthy of the Life.* What does Jesus say to Peter who will eventually claim to be the vicar of Christ? *I shall lead her, so that I will make her male, that she too may become a living spirit, resembling you males. For every woman who makes herself male will enter the Kingdom of Heaven.*

It only takes reviewing verse 106 to know what he means. *"When you make the two one"* is the key to knowing the meaning of this verse. In this case, it is a difference of gender. Jesus is not saying he can turn Mary into a male physically, but that he can lead her to know that she, too, is a *"son of the Living Father."* **In knowing she is the same as Peter, she becomes equal to Peter**.

Again, Jesus was all about seeing one where there is two. Male and female were no more two for him than were Roman and Jew or slave and master. There is no inequality in reality, related to God. We are all equally *"sons of the Living Father."* If I need to set myself apart from you, offering that you are of different Godly quality than me, then I am insisting on inequality; and whether Peter agrees with it or not, *inequality - or a sense thereof - is the single most vicious vice in the world because it only leads to destruction.*

§

So, there it is. We have finished the greatest course available to man in my opinion. Many will not agree with its simple dictums and will argue that the Jesus of Thomas is a fraud. I think it is quite adequate to say that the ones who believe the Jesus of Thomas is fraudulent are the same ones who want to keep on keeping to two. *For every female who makes herself male will enter into the Kingdom of Heaven* could also be stated in this wise. **For every male who makes himself female will enter into the Kingdom of Heaven.**

It is pretty simple, huh?

Thanks for your attention!

Francis William Bessler
April 3rd, 2009

JESUS
VIA THOMAS
COMMENTARIES

§

THE END

I'm a Wealthy Person

By
Francis William Bessler
Laramie, Wyoming
7/17/2007

REFRAIN:
I'm a wealthy person –
because I think that life is grand.
I'm a wealthy person –
because I like what I am.
I'm a wealthy person –
because I keep aware that God's inside.
I'm a wealthy person –
because in life itself, I take pride.

Wealth can come in many forms,
material and otherwise;
but no matter how it comes,
it depends upon the mind.
I feel sorry for all of those
who need a mansion to get by
because for them,
wealth is so very hard to realize.
Refrain.

So many think they need to own
material to be a king.
They think the more they control,
the more they can sing.
They think it's true for them,
but it's sure not true for me.
I find the more I control -
the less I am free.
Refrain.

I admit I do not have much,
but I've as much as I need;
and that makes me about as wealthy
as anyone can be.
Wealth is not determined
by what you have you see,
but rather what you have,
compared to what you think you need.
Refrain.

The one who is poor, then,
but lacks greed for more
is far wealthier than the rich man
who thinks he is poor.
No one needs to lack for wealth
who loves life as it is;
for such a one is always filled
and is incapable of sin.
Refrain.

I think that sin is only greed,
demanding more than you find;
and only those can sin
who are dissatisfied in mind.
So, why not join with me
and find life as is complete?
Virtue will be your companion,
as happy is your fate.
Refrain.

I'm not saying that we should
not be open to different ways.
I'm only saying that we should
be pleased with the day.
Find pleasure in what is
and adventure in what you see,
but don't neglect the present,
for the future may never be.
Refrain (multiple times if desired).

I Believe In Independence

A Poem
By
Francis William Bessler
Laramie, Wyoming
6/2005

I believe in independence,
especially from law.
I believe in independence,
starting with my thoughts.
I believe in independence
because we are all the same.
All you have I do too.
So, let us celebrate our fame.

People think they need one another
for that which they lack,
but in truth, no one lacks
that which all others have.
It is a game people of power play
to get us to agree
to join with them in some ploy
and give up being free.

Just look at the lonely
and see how they complain when alone.
That's because they pay no attention
to the beauty that they own.
No one is an island.
We all share the same humanity.
There is nothing that you have
that is not also found in me.

It is also the very same way
for each of our souls.
We are the same and all have
to attend the same rules
but the rule of the soul is
that each should be free
of other souls who try to control
and refuse them liberty.

Souls are born into bodies
to practice what they believe.
The body is only a lab
by which we can use to see –
to see what we might be doing
to other souls if we could.
The wise soul will not treat self or others
as a piece of wood.

Wood is something that humans use
to build and to mold,
but it is dead, not alive,
unlike a soul created to be bold.
When people use others as if
they were only blocks of stone,
then light turns to darkness
and souls in their bodies moan.

So, let us one and all,
pledge to see ourselves as whole,
having all the beauty of our Creator
in ourselves alone.
Let us know of our true worth
and then let us all commence
to never let others keep us
from loving our independence.

I believe in independence,
especially from law.
I believe in independence,
starting with my thoughts.
I believe in independence
because we are all the same.
All you have I do too.
So, let us celebrate our fame.

Jesus Via Mary Commentaries

§

By
Francis William Bessler
Laramie, Wyoming
- 2009 -

Introduction

§

WHO WAS JESUS? WHO IS Jesus? In all likelihood, no one knows. Many think they know, but I truly doubt that anyone does – including me. Up until rather recently in history, we have been limited to the **Gospels of Matthew, Mark, Luke, and John** and perhaps the **Epistles of such as Peter and Paul** for any testimony regarding Jesus. I grew up thinking these are the only sources about Jesus; but since 1979 or so, I became aware that there were other gospels written about Jesus. Among the other gospels written about Jesus are those of the **Apostle Thomas** and the **feminine friend of Jesus, Mary Magdalene.** Until later in my life, I had no idea there had ever been a Gospel of **Thomas or Mary** – and I am not alone. Most Christians are still unaware that there are other gospels.

1945 should be considered a very pivotal year in the history of mankind. A World War II ended in that year – and perhaps as importantly – a long hidden gospel of Jesus was discovered quite by accident in a cave off the Nile River in Egypt near a place called Nag Hammadi. That gospel – allegedly written by Thomas, one of the Twelve Apostles of Jesus – had been stored in a big jar with several other manuscripts since around the 4th Century. Why were these manuscripts hidden for all this time? Because it seems by Constantinian Edict (& Church Edict), all gospels not selected for what is known as the *BIBLE* were supposed to be destroyed. Among many works to be destroyed were the rejected works of *THE GOSPEL ACCORDING TO THOMAS* and *THE GOSPEL OF MARY.*

If it had not been for the accidental finding of the Gospel of Thomas in that cave in Egypt in 1945, personally I may have never encountered the possibility of additional gospels about Jesus; but because of that discovery by a peasant who had no idea what he had found, eventually the Gospel of Thomas would be translated from its Coptic state into many languages, including my own English. Eventually, I would become aware of not only an idea that there were others gospels written about Jesus, but I would become aware of several of the other gospels. Since my discovery of *THE GOSPEL ACCORDING TO THOMAS* in 1979, I have made it my chief source for information about Jesus. I still regard the gospels of the *BIBLE* as important, but my favorite has become the **Gospel of Thomas**. Why? Because the verses of that gospel seem to define a Jesus I would like to know much better than the others. I have written an essay type work featuring the Gospel of Thomas that I call **JESUS VIA THOMAS COMMENTARIES** (featured earlier in this work), should anyone find that useful or interesting.

In 2004, I became aware of another gospel, for the most part lost for centuries by virtue of Constantinian Edict like the Gospel of Thomas was as well. That gospel – which is the subject of this work – is what is known as ***THE GOSPEL OF MARY***. Because I find the Gospel of Mary defining Jesus in a more favorable way than the regular gospels of the ***BIBLE***, the Gospel of Mary has become my second favorite gospel. That is something, considering I did not even know it existed until 2004.

Why did Constantine, and/or his bishops, ban those gospels not selected for the ***BIBLE***? I may be wrong, but I suspect it was because he did not want to suffer any conflict that allowing rejected gospels to survive might cause. It was much simpler to allow only those gospels selected by his bishops and not only ban gospels not selected by his bishops, but command they be destroyed as well so as to leave no evidence of their prior existence. It seems to have worked quite well, too, not only for the period of time in which Constantine ruled, but for most of history since then. There has been no conflict regarding different views of Jesus because there has not been any other views – until recently.

I see the suppression of alternate sources about Jesus like a court ruling that the testimony of only certain of alleged eye witnesses should be allowed. That would be just fine if all the eye witnesses saw the same thing, but it becomes quite a travesty of justice if witnesses saw different things. If only certain testimony is allowed, think of the injustice that might be caused if testimony is only accepted from what turns out to be false witnesses. All witnesses could be sincere, even those who fail to see what really happened; but by not allowing the testimony of all of those who claim to have been eye witnesses, justice may very likely be denied.

That is what may have happened with the suppression of some of the gospels about Jesus. The result may be that we have had an inadequate rendering of Jesus for all these years. I am not saying that it is definitely so. I am only offering that it is possible, though personally, I think it is not only possible, but probable. In light of the different versions of Jesus that have now become available, it is somewhat clear to me that the real Jesus has "probably" been lost for centuries. With this work on the Gospel of Mary, I am trying to clarify the story of Jesus; though it is possible that Mary herself was a false witness of Jesus in terms of not really knowing him. On the other hand, it may be Matthew, Mark, Luke, and John who are the false witnesses; and witnesses like Thomas and Mary may be the more truthful witnesses in terms of their perceptions of Jesus may be the more accurate as reflecting the real Jesus.

When I use the word "false," I do not wish to imply "intentionally false." I only wish to imply false by virtue of the real truth. I do not doubt that Matthew, Mark, Luke, and John saw Jesus in the way they define in their works; but neither do I doubt that Thomas and Mary and others saw Jesus in the way they define in their works either. I do not wish to impugn any source as being intentionally misleading; but I do wish to suggest that misleading may have in fact occurred because the wrong gospel writers may have been embraced as knowing Jesus better than the authors eventually rejected. All we can do now is try and right the situation and maybe show Jesus in a different light.

I am under the impression the version of Mary's gospel featured here came from a Coptic (Egyptian) translation and was found in the first tractate of something called a **BERLIN GNOSTIC CODEX**. It is my understanding that this codex was acquired by a **German scholar named Dr. Carl Reinhardt from Cairo in 1896**. In the codex acquired at the time, there were three ancient works – **The Gospel of Mary, The Apocrypha of John,** and **The Sophia of Jesus Christ.** Due to subsequent World Wars I and II, the works were not translated to other languages until 1955 or so. **Mr. Marvin Meyer** – who is providing the translation I am offering below – did not offer any history as to how and where in Cairo these works were kept, prior to 1896.

Regarding **The Gospel of Mary,** perhaps there are other versions, but the Coptic version is the most complete text, though it is missing the first six manuscript pages at the beginning and four manuscript pages in the middle. Presumably, according to Marvin Meyer, **The Gospel of Mary** was originally composed in Greek, but the date and place of composition are unknown. Someone called **Karen King** has suggested that the original Gospel of Mary may have been penned in the late first or early second century, perhaps in Syria or Egypt. Again, it is assumed that the Mary of authorship is Mary Magdalene – or a disciple thereof.

I will transcribe the work as it is found in Marvin Meyer's work. The numbering of the verses below – which could be called "chapters" – are my own. Like I said, from the actual work, several pages are missing at the beginning and several in the middle. What I show as # 1 could actually be # 7 or so. I do not think it matters – just as long as you are aware that my numbers do not equate to anything in the original works.

Also, as in any translations, that which I offer below is only one version – in this case, that of Marvin Meyer. I have seen some versions that refer to the wonderful term of *child of humanity* that you will find that I love so much in my added commentary to be **son of man**. Every time I read one of these interpretations and see so much variance, I come away almost befuddled. Why Marvin Meyer would refer to a term as *child of humanity* and another would call that same term **son of man** is beyond astonishing to me. The two terms are almost worlds apart. My guess is that the translation offering **son of man** is trying to parallel **The Gospel of Mary** with other gospels that refer to Jesus as **son of man** and suggest that **The Gospel**

of Mary should be an extension of the other gospels, not a challenge thereof. I do not know that to be the case; but it is a suspicion.

As you will see, I put a lot of spiritual emphasis on the term *child of humanity* in my commentary after the verses. To change that to **son of man** is, in essence, to change it to **Jesus Christ** since Jesus referred to himself in other gospels as **son of man**. Wow! To do that is to change the entire scope and intent of using a term like *child of humanity* as far as I am concerned. I think that Jesus probably used the term – or whatever term he may have used – to represent some spiritual identity in each of us not tied to Jesus himself as Jesus; but I have seen translations that imply he meant himself.

In the end, each of us can only relate to what makes sense to us personally. I will offer the verses of **The Gospel of Mary** as I found them in Marvin Meyer's work; and then later comment on the text as presented there. In all of this, my first intent is to provide the text of the Gospel of Mary. My opinion about what that text may mean is also being provided, but far more important than my personal opinion is the text itself. My personal interpretation is not near as important as is the text itself. You can attend to my personal comments or not – though my comments will only pertain to the first verse for reasons I will state; but in any case, I hope you will choose to consider the text as significant and proceed accordingly.

Meditate on it. Make it your own, as you will.

Sincerely,

Francis William Bessler

April 22nd, 2009

1.
THE DISCIPLES DIALOGUE
WITH THE SAVIOR

"Will matter be destroyed or not?"

The savior replied, "All natures, all formed things, all creatures exist in and with each other, and they will dissolve into their own root. The nature of matter is dissolved into the root of its nature. Whoever has ears to hear should hear."

Peter said to him, "You have explained everything to us. Tell us also, what is the sin of the world?"

The savior replied, "There is no such thing as sin, but you create sin when you mingle as in adultery, and this is called sin. For this reason the good came among you, to those of every nature, in order to restore nature to its root."

He continued, "That is why you become sick and die, for [you love] what [deceives you]. Whoever has a mind should understand.

"Matter gave birth to passion that is without form, because it comes from what is contrary to nature, and then confusion arose in the whole body. That is why I told you, be of good courage. And if you are discouraged, be encouraged in the presence of the diversity of forms in nature. Whoever has ears to hear should hear."

When the blessed one said this, he greeted all of them and said, "Peace be with you. Receive my peace. Be careful that no one leads you astray by saying, 'Look here' or 'Look there.' The child of humanity is within you. Follow that. Those who seek it will find it. Go and preach the good news of the kingdom. Do not lay down any rules other than what I have given you, and do not establish law, as the lawgiver did, or you will be bound by it."

When he said this, he left them.

2.
MARY CONSOLES THE DISCIPLES AND PETER CHALLENGES MARY

The disciples were grieved. They wept profoundly and said, "How can we go to the gentiles and preach the good news of the kingdom of the child of humanity? If they did not spare him, how will we be spared?"

Mary stood up and greeted them all, and said to her brothers, "Do not weep or grieve or be in doubt, for his grace will be with you all and will protect you. Rather, let us praise his greatness, for he has prepared us and made us truly human."

When Mary said this, she turned their hearts to the good, and they began to discuss the words of the [savior].

Peter said to Mary, "Sister, we know the savior loved you more than any other woman. Tell us the words of the savior that you remember, which you know but we do not, because we have not heard them."

Mary answered and said, "What is hidden from you I shall reveal to you."

She began to speak these words to them.

She said, "I saw the master in a vision and I said to him, 'Master, I saw you today in a vision.'

"He answered and said to me, 'Blessings on you, since you did not waver when you saw me. For where the mind is, the treasure is.'

"I said to him, 'Master, how does a person see a vision, with the soul or with the spirit?'

"The savior answered and said, 'A person sees neither with the soul nor with the spirit. The mind, which is between the two, sees the vision....' "

3.
MARY RECOUNTS HER VISION OF THE SOUL'S ASCENT

"Desire said, 'I did not see you descending, but now I see you ascending. Why are you lying, since you belong to me?'

"The soul answered and said, 'I saw you, but you did not see me or know me. To you, I was only a garment, and you did not recognize me.'

"After the soul said this, she left, rejoicing greatly.

"The soul approached the third power, called ignorance. The power questioned the soul, saying, 'Where are you going? You are bound by wickedness, you are bound, so do not pass judgment.'

"The soul said, 'Why do you pass judgment on me, though I have not passed judgment? I was bound, but I have not bound. I was not recognized, but I have recognized that all is to be dissolved, both what is earthly and what is heavenly.'

"When the soul overcame the third power, she ascended and saw the fourth power. It took seven forms:

The first form is darkness,
the second, desire,
the third, ignorance,
the fourth, death wish,
the fifth, fleshly kingdom,
the sixth, foolish fleshly wisdom,
the seventh, angry person's wisdom.

"These are the seven powers of wrath.

"The powers asked the soul, 'Where are you coming from, slayer of humans, and where are you going, destroyer of realms?'

"The soul answered and said, 'What binds me is slain, what surrounds me is destroyed, my desire is gone, ignorance is dead. In a world I was freed through another world, and in an image I was freed through a heavenly image. The fetter of forgetfulness is temporary. From now on I shall rest, through the course of the time of the age, in silence.' "

4.
PETER AND ANDREW
DOUBT MARY'S WORD

When Mary said this, she became silent, since the savior had spoken this much to her.

Andrew answered and said to the brothers, "Say what you think about what she said, but I do not believe the savior said this. These teachings certainly are strange ideas."

Peter voiced similar concerns. He asked the others about the savior: "Did he really speak with a woman in private, without our knowledge? Should we all turn and listen to her? Did he prefer her to us?"

5.
LEVI SPEAKS ON BEHALF OF MARY

Then Mary wept and said to Peter, "My brother, Peter, what do you think? Do you think I made this up by myself or that I am lying about the savior?"

Levi answered and said to Peter, "Peter, you always are angry. Now I see you arguing against this woman like an adversary. If the savior made her worthy, who are you to reject her? Surely the savior knows her well. That is why he has loved her more than us.

"So, we should be ashamed and put on perfect humanity and acquire it, as he commanded us, and preach the good news, not making any rule or law other than what the savior indicated."

When [Levi said] this, they began to leave [in order to] teach and preach.

COMMENTARY:

That is all of the Gospel of Mary that author Marvin Meyer provided in his work, **The Gospels of Mary**. His was an argument that Mary Magdalene should clearly be considered one of the apostles of Jesus based on many accounts about her that seem to offer her as a favorite of Jesus. Though I may agree with Mr. Meyer's main argument, my citing of **The Gospel of Mary** is not so much to highlight Mary as it is to offer a bit more in terms of what Jesus may have taught. In his overall work, Mr. Meyer offers citations from a lot of gospels, in the *BIBLE* and outside of it, about Mary Magdalene. Her importance is tremendous as I see it, but her importance acknowledged, I am much more interested in what Jesus may have taught.

The first verse, that headed with the title *THE DISCIPLES DIALOGUE WITH THE SAVIOR,* seems to be the one and only verse that might be attributed to a pre-death Jesus. The others seem to amount to reflections of Mary and the others after the death of Jesus about their understanding of Jesus and what he may have taught. I find myself intrigued with the first verse because of its potential of being some actual words of Jesus during his life – not to say they were actual words for sure, but only potentially so. On the other hand, verses two through five are much less intriguing to me because they are ponderings about experiences that Mary Magdalene may have had after the death of Jesus. Perhaps they have some validity in a general sense, but I prefer to leave them to and with Mary.

To be truthful, however, I find paranormal experiences quite suspect because one can never be sure who the ghostly sender of a message is. In this case, Mary Magdalene may have been positive that one who sent her a vision was Jesus, but any ghost or spirit who might be trying to communicate with one who is "expecting" some paranormal visit – or visit from a ghost – would probably be smart enough to disguise him or her or itself enough to not be suspected as not being Jesus. Thus, once in, a paranormal ghost could mislead as much as lead. It is because of this possibility that I suspect any ghost for having anything worthwhile hearing.

It is offered in several of the gospels that Jesus warned us against false pretensions in his name – or using his name. Given this warning, I even suspect the alleged vision of Jesus to his mother and Mary Magdalene and the disciples of Jesus may have been fraudulent on the part of some ghost who may have seen an opportunity to gain a foothold. Visions for me are very suspect – any of them – because of an uncertainty as to their origin.

How, for instance, could Saul of Tarsus be sure the spirit who visited him on the road to Damascus was not a pretender? Saul had not known Jesus. I find it all too likely that a pretender spirit could have visited Saul and turned him into Paul, claiming to be Jesus. Who could know different? This is an example of a possible mislead by a fraudulent spirit or ghost or community of ghosts. The visions as recorded in the famed **Book of Revelations** of the *BIBLE* are likewise suspect for their being advanced after the death of Jesus about Jesus. Who is to say that deceitful ghosts are not the real authors of the visions offered in that work too? It is just too uncertain to trust any of these type communications. So, I try to avoid them.

It is also possible that a vision of another that someone has comes strictly from within the person having the vision. In that case, it is a purely subjective experience and may only be one suggesting to him or herself something of considered importance – much like a dream, if not a version of a dream. Dreams are much too subjective for me to take seriously – be they of the unconscious sleeping variety or the perhaps wide awake visionary variety. I know very little about either phenomenon – and choose to ignore any message supposedly told through them.

For me, verses two through five of **The Gospel of Mary** come under the umbrella of uncertain for potential false paranormal links – or subjective visioning or dreaming. **I am not saying they are false. I am only saying I do not want to trust them.** It is hard enough trying to make sense of personal recollections of things allegedly said. I will leave all the visionary and post death happenings claimed of Jesus to those who have them – at least in this work. Omitting post-death of Jesus verses of **The Gospel of Mary,** however, I have but one verse of that gospel to try and interpret.

CREATURES & MATTER

That one verse (1) begins with a discussion of matter. Jesus is asked *will matter be destroyed or not?* **He answers -** *All natures, all formed things, all creatures exist in and with each other, and they will dissolve into their own root. The nature of matter is dissolved into the root of its nature. Whoever has ears to hear should hear.*

I think we need to keep in mind that the English words and English translation may not do the actual words of Jesus justice, but in general, I get from this part of the verse that Jesus thinks that all creatures are like a family of beings, existing in and with each other. I like this idea very much and relate to it. I like to think of myself as a brother to the rose and the rose as a sister to me. I like to think of everything I can see as being one of my siblings. From the sounds of the first words of this verse, Jesus agreed with that kind of thinking.

Besides my being a spiritual sibling of all things and all things being spiritual siblings of mine, Jesus offers that all things will dissolve into their own roots. What can he mean by that, if he really said it? I do not know. This is a part of the verse that has no clear answers for me. What does it mean "to dissolve into a root"? If it means that from dust I was and to dust I will return, that makes a lot of sense. My body or body parts will return to their source of origin, back to the matter from which they sprang. I have no problem with that. Essentially, however, the matter of my being will not be destroyed. Only that which is formed of the matter will cease and return to its root.

Importantly in this mini discussion of life and matter, however, I am taken by how casual this process probably is for Jesus. It's only a matter of course, not a decision about good and evil. I like that. Personally, I see no evil in life or any part of any process of life. All processes in life or within life and life itself are a mystery and a miracle for me. I stand in awe of it all; but standing in awe of it, I do not need to understand it. Jesus may have understood a lot more than I do or can about the process of life. I really cannot go there. Thus, the first part of this verse is wonderfully comforting to me, as if offering sanctity to the whole process of life whatever that process is; but personally, I can't go much beyond a sense of awe in this part of the discussion. It makes a lot of sense to me that things return to their root – or that flesh and life return to the base matter from which they sprang to life. Perhaps that is all that Jesus is saying here.

It is worthwhile to speculate, though, that Jesus is offering that at the conclusion of life – at least of a human being – the body will "dissolve" into its particular origin – matter - and the soul will "dissolve" (or return) to its original state before it incarnated into body – as soul by itself. In any case, with death, all things return to some original state before any life as composed of parts began in the first place. The body goes back to being matter – or if you wish, dust; and the soul goes back to whatever it was – and maybe wherever it was – before it entered a body in the first place. *(A)ll creatures exist in and with each other, and they will dissolve into their own root* – could only mean that at the time of death of a human being, matter (or body) will return to matter and soul will return to soul (without body). Personally, that is my belief – whether Jesus intended it as definition in this stated quote or not.

ALL ABOUT SIN

Next, however, Peter asks Jesus about sin. He wants to know, what is the sin of the world? Jesus answered - *There is no such thing as sin, but you create sin when you mingle as in adultery, and this is called sin. For this reason the good came among you, to those of every nature, in order to restore nature to its root.*

I think Jesus is offering that there is no sin in nature, as nature itself is formed – or as natural things exist in life; however, we *create sin* for ourselves when we mingle, perhaps only in erratic ways. It could be taken that Jesus offers that we see ourselves in sin when we mingle improperly or that we actually sin when we mingle improperly.

Going at this from my own perspective, I feel that I have wronged in life or have committed wrong only when I view what I do as somehow distracting from a sense of oneness or unity, especially with God, but also with persons. I sin – if you want to call it that – when I do something either with no purpose in mind or a purpose of hurting another or knowing that I will hurt them. In that sense, deviating from my own intent and good **creates sin** for me. For the most part, when I do sin – or fail the unity test – it is with another. Thus, it would make sense that I would normally **create sin** mostly in mingling with others.

Very importantly, however, I hear Jesus flatly denying that there is sin in nature itself. He said **there is no such thing as sin** in terms of somehow existing by itself in nature or life or whatever.

This is very important because it denies so called **evil regions** or **evil places** or **evil things**. In my mind, this is somewhat confronting to the traditional notion that humans **inherit sin**. I hear Jesus saying we cannot **inherit sin**. We can only **create** it. That is to say that no one is **born helpless** or **born defective**. Perhaps we are born within attitudes of helplessness or defectiveness, but that helplessness or defectiveness is not part of our nature per se. Our natures are, in fact, perfect. It is only by seeing them imperfect that we take upon ourselves a sense of imperfection or defectiveness.

I was brought up with the idea that Jesus came into life to **take away my sin**. According to this mini discussion of sin, that could not be. I have no sin in me to be taken away by anyone. How could Jesus take away that which I do not have? If by sin is meant **improper mingling** with others – as it seems Jesus defines it – then the only way I could become sinless is by stopping the improper mingling. How could Jesus be responsible for that? Of course, he can't. Thus, it would seem that it could not be that Jesus could take away a sin. Now, we are getting down to a real issue of life. In this verse, I hear Jesus flatly denying that he could – or anyone can – take away sin. From the perspective of inheriting sin, such is impossible; and from the perspective of improper mingling, only I can stop that. Thus, Jesus is resolved from having to resolve sin in me.

Of course it could be argued that someone could aid another in stopping their sin or sinful behavior. In that sense, yes, you could aid me in the **removal of a sin**. In that light, yes, Jesus could be considered to provide the insight that allows me to take action and dissolve or resolve my own sin; but in the end, it is I who must resolve the sin – not Jesus or anyone else.

Let us finish this part of the verse. It continues. Let's repeat the entire statement: *There is no such thing as sin, but you create sin when you mingle as in adultery, and this is called sin. For this reason the good came among you, to those of every nature, in order to restore nature to its root.*

Jesus seems to offer that improper mingling is related to adultery. How could this be? Again, looking from my own sense of comfort, I feel best when I am independent, when I feel a sense of wholesomeness all my own – or feel that I am individually wholesome. Adultery goes against that sense of individual wholesomeness. It suggests that I am not complete unto myself to have need of it. So, from a standpoint of individual integrity or sense of individual wholesomeness, any adultery or dependence on another for personal satisfaction could indeed ***create* sin** for me.

That is not to say I should refrain from any mingling with others. It is only to say that I should allow no mingling that detracts from an individual sense of worth or completion. Sure, I have to mingle sexually to procreate. That's fine – as long as I do not mingle sexually for reasons of needing it to feel complete. I realize that is a bit of a slippery ledge; but the truth of it should be clear, even if it might seem difficult.

A Mini Discussion of Sex & Sin

Perhaps we are getting ahead of ourselves by talking about sex now; but since we are chatting about sin and sin is often equated to sex, it might be a good idea to introduce a discussion of it.

I am not much interested in how the world has looked at sex, related to sin. So I prefer to start this discussion as if no history preceded me. Jesus offers that sin is **improper mingling** – though he did not say it that way exactly. He said, ***when you mingle as in adultery, this is called sin.*** I think it is fair enough to call such "mingling" as "improper." Thus I paraphrase ***mingle as in adultery*** as **improper mingling.**

Be that as it may, when are things sexual improper mingling? The wonderful thing about Jesus is that he accented personal responsibility in deciding the issues of life. So, to start, improper mingling in sex can only be decided by the party or parties involved.

Allowing myself to be personal, I love sex. I see it on the equal of eating or drinking or sleeping. I love all those things too. Sex, for me, though, is as much of the mind as the body, as much of the soul as the flesh. Trying to decide all issues of any worth on a spiritual plain, that is how it might affect my soul, I decide sex on the very platform that Jesus offered we should conduct life – **refraining from improper mingling.** Of course, it is to each his or her own, though churches down through history have tried more in the area of sex to impose some general standards. But for me, sex is no more or less important than anything else in life. Upon entering a relationship, I ask myself, is the soul of a potential partner in step with me? If the answer is yes, then sex with that person is a possibility. If it is no, then sex is out of the question.

It is really simple – as long as you let your mind decide the issue and not your body. I love my body because I think it is a Natural and Godly gift in terms of both Nature and God are allowing me to possess it. My body is a companion to my soul. I think it was that way for Jesus too. If you do not see your body as a companion to your soul, I can imagine life's issues are far more complicated than they are for me; but loving myself in my soul and in my soul's current home – my body – I am almost always in delight.

I have another advantage, though, too, over almost everyone I know. I am constantly aware that I am really two - not one - in a manner of speaking. My soul and my body make me two. In my case, my soul and my body are quite in love, as it were. My soul looks toward my body for its delight; and my body is always there to respond to the wishes of my soul. Now, if you are one who has a war going on inside between body and soul, then I suppose you would see things much different than I.

Getting back to our discussion of sex and sin, and basing sin on **improper mingling**, I cannot treat my body as anything different than another person. I cannot assume my body wants to do any given thing. It always depends on its state and its health. For me to impose something on my body – as for instance, a drug – I have to consider the possible impact before I can take it. To take a drug for my body without my soul (or mind) in concurrence is to be guilty of **improper mingling** between soul and body. Even though I am alone in the decision, if my soul does something that knowingly will hurt the body and the companionship between soul and body, sin is the result. I will have just exacted a state of **improper mingling** between my soul and body.

In my case, my body and my soul have a thing going between them in the sensual arena. I am not sure it could be called sexual, but it certainly is as good as sex if it is not sex. It is as if my soul wants to know the sensual delights of the body. So I allow my body to comply with my soul's wishes, though I will admit I don't do much in the way of exotic. A little exotic now and then might be ok, but for the most part, my soul is just glad to have a good body for a home. By looking in the mirror at my body, my soul gets the message that it chose well. By enjoying a shower, my body tells my soul that it chose well. I am always in touch with who and what I am because I chose life for the experience.

That does not mean I always choose well. I may try something that I expect to enhance my body; but now and then, it does not work out. To continue some practice by taking too much of a chance of hurting my body, my soul cries out – **improper mingling! Stop!** I try to listen to my body, but I must admit I do have a weakness for sweets. Now and then I will overdo and have to put up with an awful state of heartburn. When that happens, my soul cries out – **I told you to stop. Now as your soul I have to sit inside of you and experience something other than joy.** So, my soul gives my body a good whipping and I am off to the races again.

I may die of a heart attack while doing what I think is good for my body. It happens. My soul has to take leave of my body eventually, anyway; but to do something that I know will end in a heart attack and abort the life my soul wants to love is a really big issue of **improper mingling**. I think that if people were aware of their own soul/body companionship, they would take life much more seriously and realize that even alone, one can sin by doing what is not good for the continuation of life.

Having said that, if I were to find tomorrow I had some terrible illness that might be treatable, I may well decide to pack it in anyway. I would have a grand discussion with my soul and my body; and if my soul decided it is time to go – I might do it. Who knows? If my body became an unacceptable companion for my soul, I may decide to allow the separation – thanking my body for a truly wonderful temporary experience.

I could exist on an island and only have to deal with myself; but given most reality, one has to deal with others too. I use the same precedence I use in dealing with my soul and body in determining my extra personal relationships too. In the area of sex, I always have to ask a potential partner about it to go forward with it; and a potential partner must always ask me about sex to go forward with it. If I should not ask and simply assume willingness on the part of a partner, then I am guilty of **improper mingling**. If a partner does not ask and simply assumes it would be right, then I am also guilty of **improper mingling** if I allow her - her way.

Again, every person must decide their own comfort level with any dealings in life. It should be a personal responsibility. I am not offering that others should adopt my own standard, but personally I will allow sex only with a partner who shares my love for life in the way I enjoy it. For starters, that means God must be a prime consideration. I will not allow sex with anyone who does not exclaim **Oh God!** during the act and mean it. I am personally not interested in dallying in bed with anyone who does not share my love for God and Life.

When the **Oh God!** becomes missing in a sexual relationship for me, sex is something I forbid. If I start out with a relationship and the **Oh God!** seems to be part of the experience, I can go forward with it; but once a partner drops the **Oh God!**, the act changes and I will no longer go forward with it. Why? Because the relationship will have changed to be an **improper mingling** thing.

Improper mingling, for me, is doing anything that distracts my soul from its goal in life of loving life and God in everything I do. If I have a partner who does not see in me a brother in God, then I feel distracted. Perhaps others can do a mind over matter thing; but it does not work for me. Each one must decide on their own what works for them; and that is the key in this discussion of sin. Stated as the Jesus of Mary states it, we *create sin* when we allow ourselves to be distracted from our goals in life. It is not only up to each person to decide their own goals, free only to consult as the soul it is, but it is also up to each person to decide if an act is a distraction toward meeting a goal. I cannot decide sin for you; and you cannot decide sin for me. My virtue could be your sin and my sin your virtue. Ideally, that is the way it should be.

GOOD SOULS –LIVING TO HELP TRAPPED SOULS

Then Jesus said: *For this reason the good came among you, to those of every nature, in order to restore nature to its root*. What could he have meant by that? Who are the good who came among us? I think that is a reference to souls with a sense of individual wholesomeness being born into the world to aid others without such a sense. That implies reincarnation. That implies that some of us come into the world without a proper sense of individual integrity or wholesomeness and others are born into the world with a proper sense of integrity. Jesus did not say – for that reason, I came into the world. He said – for that reason, the good came into the world, implying a community of good souls. At least, that is how I see it.

To continue, Jesus said the good came into the world *to those of every nature, in order to restore nature to its root*. What did he mean by *to those of every nature?* Perhaps he was talking about attitudes. Maybe it should have been stated – to those of every attitude. But that could only mean to those of every bad attitude or every unkind attitude or "un-good attitude." But why? *In order to restore nature to its root.* If he really meant nature in general, that implies nature has somehow lost its way in order to need restoring.

We have already determined that Jesus did not believe that there is sin in nature itself. So we know he could not have meant that nature itself needs restoring. My answer to that is that if nature itself does not need restored, then it must be our perception of nature that needs restored or corrected. Maybe some of us have wandered from a proper perspective of nature – perhaps by becoming to believe there is sin in nature – and the good who have a proper perspective are born into the world to help us who have wandered back to a proper perspective of seeing nature and everything in nature as intrinsically good. Now, that makes one heck of a lot of sense. Doesn't it?

Of course if you do not believe in reincarnation and the previous existence of souls prior to any incarnation, then that makes no sense. Then you are left to trying to explain people being bad by virtue of inheriting bad natures or bad bodies or bad spirits or whatever. That seems to me to be the approach that much traditional religion has taken. People are not born with personal dispositions. They are born with natural dispositions and everyone is tainted by nature – or a fallen nature. As I see it, however, the Jesus of Mary did not believe in the possibility of a tainted nature. He said there is no such thing as sin in terms of nature itself. He said that we only *"create sin"* by doing stupid things – like adultery. Am I not right?

Given that reincarnation is likely, however, it all makes sense. If souls exist prior to incarnating, they must have had previous experiences. Upon reincarnation, whatever attitudes they had in a last life could only be inherited in a current life. In that sense, some souls could **inherit the sin of their fathers**, but "their fathers" are really only themselves since they have really inherited themselves in terms of being born again with the same attitude of their previous death. A lot of this makes sense from that point of view. Perhaps Jesus said, the good came among us in order to restore us to a proper path. In that light, yes, Jesus could be seen as a savior – as could all of those good souls that Jesus talks about in this verse. It makes a lot of sense to me, given that we are talking about wayward souls and not wayward natures.

In any discussion of life – be it about Jesus or anything – I take note that I may not be getting it right. I try to present my arguments within a scope of trying to make sense of things. I have no revelation to assure me that anything I think is right; but by thinking about things, at least I do not leave myself completely naked with no defenses from thought onslaughts of others. None of us know for sure about anything that is of a spiritual or transparent nature. We are all guessing. In many cases, the thoughtful are blind; in others, perhaps, there is clearer vision. All we can do is try and see as clearly as we can and leave as little to the supposed insights of others as possible. It is in this light that I even attempt to interpret what any wise man may have said. In the end, if it makes sense, it might be right; but if it makes no sense whatever, then it should be suspect.

SIN – PRECEDENCE FOR ILLNESS

Assuming our pondering makes any sense whatever, let's continue with the first verse. Jesus then said: ***That is why you become sick and die, for [you love] what [deceives you]. Whoever has a mind should understand.*** I think Jesus is implying that sickness and death, though not all death of course, results from confusion. This is a continuation of the theme of our creating sin for ourselves with improper mingling. Because we commit sin, we become sick – and with some sickness, the end is death. Thus, our deaths can be attributed to sin – in some cases. Jesus died. Theoretically, he had no sin. So all death can not be attributed to sin; but that death which results from avoidable sickness, I guess, can.

That makes sense. Look at the current **AIDS** sickness. It is one sickness that clearly results from **improper mingling**. Though there are exceptions, many **AIDS** victims become sick because they mingle and pass on entities in some fashion that result in sickness. Without such mingling, this sickness would not happen; and perhaps it is true with most sickness. Maybe by improper mingling with each other, we share germs and agents that cause our health to break down. The more independent each of us is, it stands to reason, the less likely we can catch a disease by improper mingling.

This is not to say we should not mingle at all; but I think it is a strong statement for loving the solitary as much as possible. Personally I love to mingle with others, but never to the detriment of my own sense of worth. If I am exposed to a situation that serves to undermine my sense of integrity, this kid is gone – not only to preserve my own soulful and mindful health, but to allow others to go on their path as they choose as well.

I do believe Jesus was one smart guy. He knew how important it is to stand alone and not depend on another for one's worth. He tried to teach that independence to all; and yet, I think he was misunderstood. I think we have concluded that for his independence he was seen as stronger than any of us can be. He did not depend on others. For that, he was made a God because only Gods can be independent. We missed the tale of his life if we conclude that. At least, I think we do.

Jesus could have engaged in improper mingling with others, but he didn't. Why? Because he did not have any need of mingling to prove his own worth. He was strong, but his strength was not without reason – or above reason. We have made him a God because we have failed to understand his wisdom; but his wisdom can be and should be general. No man has any monopoly on what is right. Jesus had no monopoly on having a clear vision of life. We can all have his vision – if we only learn to admit our individual worth.

Why are we individually worthy? Because God is in us all. Jesus has nothing to do with God being in us all – including himself. That is just the way it is. Jesus only recognized God – or The Father – is in us all. Jesus only recognized that we all come from God. We can all recognize that; and by so doing, see ourselves as the individually worthy we really are. None of us are born, lacking God. We all have God in us. How can we know that?

By a simple process of deduction reasoning – or induction reasoning.

We can deduce that an Infinite God must be in each individual because God, being Everywhere, has to be in each entity. Flipping the logic, we can induce that we are all in God for the same reason. If God is everywhere, as It must be to be Infinite, then all must be in God and God must be in all. It is really simple.

In **The Gospel of Thomas,** Verse 3, Jesus says that *the Kingdom of the Father is inside of us and outside of us.* Jesus was aware of the omnipresence of God. I think it is that thought that provided the basis of his courage and his confidence. I say that because it is the thought that has provided the basis of whatever courage and confidence I have had in life too. In not having to struggle with the possibility of being shy of God, Jesus and I and anyone can handle the various issues of life with confidence. Knowing God is in us, we can not be deceived to believe that we need God. Knowing we do not need to attain a God we already have, no one can lead us astray by promising God via some saving exercise.

To know of the idea of omnipresence of God and celebrate it on a constant basis is the path to solitary perfection – or knowing solitary perfection. It is not our knowing it that makes it so. It is so whether we know it or not; but if we do not know it, we will not act like it; and if we do not act like it, then confusion and illness and sometimes death results.

ABOUT MATTER & PASSION

Let's continue with the verse. We are getting into deep waters now, but some of it is easy. Jesus said: *Matter gave birth to passion that is without form, because it comes from what is contrary to nature, and then confusion arose in the whole body. That is why I told you, be of good courage. And if you are discouraged, be encouraged in the presence of the diversity of forms in nature. Whoever has ears to hear should hear.*

Matter gave birth to passion that is without form. What did he mean by that? I guess it's to say that passion could not be if it were not for matter. It is certainly an interesting thought for me. I am not sure what to make of it, though. Passion comes from matter or what is material. I guess that is to say that passion does not comes from what is immaterial. Why would that be important anyway? So what? Who knows about the immaterial – or perhaps that which can be called **spiritual?**

I have always believed that the soul – which might be considered **spiritual** – comes into the body or takes residence in a body for a time. Why would a soul do that? Perhaps it is because of that *passion* that arises out of the material. I guess souls want to use that passion and can't have it in their own form. I would suspect the same. This passion that comes from the material is good, but *it comes from what is contrary to nature* if we are to believe this verse. What would Jesus mean by that – passion being contrary to nature?

What is nature? No one really knows the answer to that. We are all in nature, but none of us really know what it is. It just is, that's all. Personally, I think nature should be capitalized because for me, **Nature includes All** – all of the so called **spiritual** and all of the material. I think only a fool will try to analyze Nature per se. We are in it. What does it matter how we arrived within it? It should be for us to be grateful for being in it and pretty much let it go at that.

Still, this verse does intrigue me. I think it does have some real meaning. How could passion that comes from the material be contrary to Nature when the material exists within Nature? It's confusing. Isn't it? Come to think about it, Jesus admits this – he said *and then confusion arose in the whole body.* But then he offered that we should not let our confusion discourage us. We can't figure it out – at least not mere mortals like me. I am quite happy being a mortal and I do not have to have all the answers to lead a good life. And Jesus would agree, for after he said that I would be confused, he said, *be encouraged in the presence of the diversity of forms in nature.* Never mind having to understand it. Just look at the diversity within Nature and be happy with that. Why not? I am part of that wonderful diversity. So why not be happy with that? Right?

In other words, I think Jesus is telling us that we should celebrate life for the diversity of forms within it. Look at the diversity of things, he offers, to note how well you fit in as one of the diverse forms. Look at a butterfly and be glad and be joyful. Look at a deer and be glad and be joyful. Look at a marigold and be glad and be joyful. Look at yourself and be glad and be joyful.

I know it has worked that way with me. If I find myself feeling down with myself, all I have to do is look around me and take in the mystery around me. Then knowing I am one of the mysterious, I want to jump ten feet high for joy. Look at the diversity about you, Jesus says, and find courage and joy in life. It is really easy to do that if you just take a moment and embrace yourself within the tremendous diversity of all.

I think, too, it is quite likely that Jesus did not understand it either. He could well have been one like me just speculating about things; but when he offered this "opinion" to others, he had already conjectured for some time about the matter. So it could have given the appearance that he had never been in doubt. I suspect, however, he had been in doubt and had resolved the confusion he encountered by looking out at Nature and concluding as he concludes here – **what does it matter? Let me be happy for being part of the diversity of it all.** And thus, later, when he had an opportunity to share his conclusion with others, he was ready. I think that is the way it happened. I do not think that Jesus was God in any way different than anyone else just because he seemed to answer with some degree of certainty. I think he seemed certain simply because he had thought about it all before where most of his audience had not.

I think it is also good to keep in mind that Jesus has been made a God because of the power associated with that. Jesus has been made a being of wisdom and of miracles that no other human has had mostly to make him a God so that those associated with Jesus can assume power because Gods have power.

It is fairly clear upon review that all that Jesus is purported to have done he did not do. Just look at the miracles of the regular Gospels. All those Gospels report Jesus performing miracles, but note that the greatest miracle of them all is only reported by one of the Gospel writers – John. All the Gospels show Jesus as superhuman, but only John tells of Lazarus being raised from the dead. If that miracle had really happened, you can be sure that Matthew, Mark, and Luke would have reported it. All three wrote their Gospels long before John and omitted it. Why? Because they did not know of it or about it. How could they not know about the greatest miracle of all time? The only reasonable answer – because it did not really happen and only Dear John contrived it.

What that shows, however, is that a lot of what is claimed for Jesus may not have really happened. How many of the miracles claimed for Jesus really occurred? No one knows and no one can know because once one lie is told, all credibility is lost. Isn't it?

What happens when credibility is lost? What happens to the great speech that John has Jesus offering than none of the other Gospels do? What happens with the verse upon which most of traditional Christianity is based – *I am the vine and you are the branches?* What happens to that little gem when it becomes known that John may have contrived that to gain power or to be associated with power just as he contrived the raising of Lazarus from the dead in order to gain power or become associated with power? It all goes down the drain. No Lazarus – No God. No vine – no branches. **No God and no branches of the vine of Jesus – no power.**

But that does not mean Jesus did not live just because lies were probably told about him. It only means that those who told the lies either did not know Jesus well enough to know they were lies or wanted to use Jesus to gain power for themselves. Take your pick. Almost for sure since only the last Gospel writer of the *BIBLE* told about Lazarus, the tale of Lazarus being raised from the dead is probably fiction – and so is anything else reported in John. If he told one tall tale, he probably told all sort of tall tales, including, of course, the *I am the vine and you are the branches* jewel upon which most of traditional Christianity is based.

In all likelihood, Jesus was made a God because he may have seemed one for his seeming understanding of the world. Only Gods can understand. If Jesus understood, he had to be a God. Accordingly, if Jesus is a God, then it should be OK to attribute all sort of miracles to him even though those miracles are fable. What would it hurt?

I do not doubt that even John saw Jesus as a God because he wanted to be associated with power. We all do, I guess, until we come to realize that power is not what wisdom is all about. **Wisdom is not about power. It is about accepting ourselves within the realm of Nature.** It is not about becoming Nature and becoming powerful like Nature. It is about becoming comfortable with being a son of Nature, a child of Nature; and that discussion is just ahead. I think Jesus had thought about that a lot before he started what is called his "public ministry." He went into that ministry well prepared with answers he had found from his own personal search; but he probably never intended to be made a God for that knowledge or understanding.

THE KINGDOM OF GOD –HERE & NOW!

Then Mary Magdalene, if that's really the author of this gospel, says that *when the blessed one said this, he greeted all of them and said, "Peace be with you. Receive my peace. Be careful that no one leads you astray by saying, 'Look here' or 'Look there.' The child of humanity is within you. Follow that. Those who seek it will find it. Go and preach the good news of the kingdom. Do not lay down any rules other than what I have given you, and do not establish law, as the lawgiver did, or you will be bound by it." When he said this, he left them.* Presumably, the reference to *he left them* refers to the death of Jesus.

I think he is telling us to never mind if we have not understood what my little brain has had a hard time pondering.

Don't let anyone lead you astray, he says. Don't be deceived if one says – Look over here, I have the answers – or Look over there. Look at yourselves, he said. Look for the ***child of humanity*** within you. ***Those who seek it will find it,*** he says. That, in essence, becomes the rule I should follow – respect for the ***child of humanity*** within.

Once again, to repeat the warning of Jesus. Mary says he said: ***Be careful that no one leads you astray by saying, 'Look here' or 'Look there.'*** In **The Gospel of Thomas,** the warning is stated like this: Verse 113: ***His disciples said to Him: When will the Kingdom come? \<Jesus said:\> It will not come by expectation; they will not say: "See, here" or: "See, there." But the Kingdom of the Father is spread upon the earth and men do not see it.***

I suspect we have failed as a Christian world - and a religious world, in general - to take heed of those warnings because we have been deluged since the time of Jesus with prognosticators warning us about the kingdom coming now or then or soon or whatever. Strangely, though we were warned and it was spelled out by Jesus, we have taken the Kingdom to mean something to come later when as Jesus says in the Gospel of Thomas that the Kingdom is already here, ***spread about the earth and men do not see it.*** The powers that be, however, have nothing to gain by us thinking the Kingdom has come and is here. To keep us in their control, the Kingdom must always be future so that the prospects of a future reward can always be available as a motivation for some controlled behavior. **What is so sad**

**about this is that we were warned about it happening –
and we still fall for the claims of a future Kingdom.**

SEEKING THE *CHILD OF HUMANITY*

Anyway, with the Kingdom of the Father now present, I am
given to believe that I will be alright if I just concentrate on
this theme that Jesus calls the ***child of humanity***. What exactly is this image of spirituality that Jesus calls the ***child of
humanity*** within us? Each of us must answer that for ourselves, but for me, it is nothing more than humanity itself.
It is not, as one translator I read, intended to refer to Jesus.
That translator (from a web site called **The Gnostic Society
Library)** substituted the term **son of man** for what Marvin
Meyer calls ***child of humanity***. I repeat my introductory
statement on that matter. It is Humanity that is the lofty
thing we should admire – and each of us as human within
that. The ***child of humanity*** is really the child of God. It is
only that humanity is a child or a progeny of God. **It is not
to look for the Jesus in me, as some might think, but to
look for that which is common between Jesus and me –
our humanity. At least, it seems so to me.**

It does not mean for me to look for the kid in me, either,
but to look at my humanity as the child of God. Can anyone imagine a greater celebration than to celebrate what
we are? That is what Jesus meant, I think. The ***child of
humanity*** is a Jesus expression that says that humanity is a

child. Jesus tried to teach that we should pay no attention to those who try to defame humanity or ourselves within humanity. People too often fail to understand that. It is a very simple concept and no concept is more important than our loving the humanity which is a child of God.

In other gospels, Jesus called himself the **son of man**. By that, I think he was trying to offer what a wonderful thing it is to be a human – a son of man, a daughter of man, a child that is human. I shake my head at people overlooking this wonderful idea and trying to diminish what we are as human by attaching impersonal sin to us – as if humanity by itself is less than lovable. Jesus tried so hard to elevate, not mankind, but our vision of mankind, in terms of asking us to realize that humanity is miraculous; and yet so many people look toward Jesus as claiming to perfect humanity. Not so! **Humanity was perfect before Jesus, during the life of Jesus, and after Jesus. Jesus had nothing to do with that perfection.** He only offered that it is perfect. His image of *child of humanity* is in my opinion the most misunderstood notion ever offered our humanity in the name of religion.

I suspect that Jesus may have called himself a **son of man**, too, in order to clarify that he was not the God that some of them thought him to be. It was as if to say, **Look, I am no more God than you are. I am man like you. I am a son of man like you. Do not make me a God; for if you do, you will be overlooking your own glory and your own power of peace.** If you make me different than you, then you will lose sight of becoming like me in terms of being comfortable with life. You come to me thinking you have a sin; but there is no sin in your natures. There is only sin in your dealings with one another if you allow yourselves to be distracted from your worth by thinking you need each other to be sacred.

What is the "rule" that Jesus supposedly offered as the only rule we need to attend? Again, though it can be translated as love of God and love of man and love of self because God is in them all, it can very succinctly be stated as Jesus states it – respecting the ***child of humanity***. All law and all rule beyond that is not only useless, as Jesus would offer, but contrary to a Jesus kind of virtue.

Laws – Bad for the Soul

He said, **"do not make any more laws and regulations"** other than the rule of adhering to the ***child of humanity*** within you; but Christianity has done just the opposite. It has created as many laws and regulations as did its forefather – Judaism. That is precisely what Jesus forbade; and yet church fathers, notably Peter and his successors, have marched on making law after law and claiming that Jesus authorized them and authorizes them to do so. Commandment kind of law does nothing to enhance the soul. In my opinion, those who believe it does enhance the soul have no understanding and real appreciation of Jesus.

In Mary, as in Thomas, Peter is presented as someone who does not understand the teachings of Jesus and offers resistance. In the Gospel of Mary, his misunderstanding is of the ideal of ***child of humanity*** – or simply loving humanity as divine (Divine) – but in the biblical gospels, he puts himself above a mere rule of love and asserts himself as a legitimate law giver. Jesus said, ***Do not lay down any rules other than what I have given you, and do not establish law, as the lawgiver did, or you will be bound by it.***"

Jesus may have been referencing Moses and any other person who has tried to mitigate the rule of love with an alleged law of God; but I think it is just as clear that true Christians should pay no more attention to present and future law givers than Jesus did to previous law givers. As Jesus may have stated in the statement about not establishing law, what many do not understand is that to submit to any law is to be bound by it – regardless of a law being worthy or unworthy. Jesus warned us not to establish law because of the impact of it in terms of binding us.

Now, binding by law is just fine for those who want to control us, but it may be totally contrary to those who sincerely want to do right. Laws can be the single most dangerous impediment to the maturity of a soul. Jesus understood that and warned against it; but it seems to me we have ignored his warnings because Christian history is full of what might be called law givers using law to intimidate others into submission.

I think that the danger of law to suppress individual freedom has been demonstrated time after time in history. No greater example of that is the story of Galileo being required to submit to the law giver of his time. Here was a man that time has demonstrated was right; and he was intimidated by Christian lawmen via a Christian hierarchy which claimed their authority was God given.

Look what happened to Galileo. He did not agree with the law that bid that he had to renounce his claim that the Earth revolves around the Sun but he still went along with it. In spite of not believing in the law that was passed to reprimand him for what was considered heresy, he submitted to it. He believed that the lawmen in his case had divine authority over him – and like Jesus offered in the verse warning against law, because he believed in the authority of the lawmen in question, he was bound by their law. In effect, because he believed that others could make divine laws, inspired by God, even though the law was, in fact, unreal, he was still bound by it.

And there it is. The terribly sad thing about it all is that no law is necessary to decide morality – in terms of laws intended to guide a soul to God. Because of the Infinite Everywhere Presence of God, All are already in God and God is already in every soul. Any law that might be specified as some act necessary to gain access to God is on its face, invalid. **Religious Law Is Nonsense.** Jesus knew this; but he also knew that those who might find religious law somehow relevant are automatically bound by it – no matter how untrue in reality it might be.

In essence, I think that Jesus taught that our natures are good – and as long as we see ourselves as whole and without need of aid by another to attain meaning and sanctity, all is well. It is when we insist that mingling and membership is a necessity to attain sanctity and divinity that we create sin for ourselves. There is no sin in our natures, however. The good came among us, Jesus said, to try to get us to realize our individual perfection. He said, look to your nature to find your meaning. Look to the ***child of humanity*** or the **solitary human experience** to know the good within you.

The emphasis here should be on **solitary**. Social human experience may actually prove harmful to a soul if the social interaction is considered necessary for individual perfection; but solitary human experience intended as an expression of individual wholesomeness can only always be right. Like Jesus may have argued, though there is no sin in any of our natures, we may well create sin for ourselves if we require mingling and membership with others as a requirement for individual perfection.

JESUS – NOT A SAVIOR (OR MESSIAH)! ONLY A JOURNEYMAN WITH A MESSAGE OF FREEDOM

We have already touched on it, but I think this notion of the good coming among us seems to be an underlying message in all the gospels. I think it means that many who reside as souls who have realized their own sanctity by virtue of realizing that God is within them incarnate in order to help other souls realize the ideal of individual sanctity too. Jesus was probably one of those who incarnated to help others escape from the various prisons of self denunciation. Unfortunately, he has been viewed as commanding the very self denunciation that is contrary to health of soul. He has been viewed as offering that others can find meaning only through him. In my opinion, nothing is further from the truth.

It would be like my telling others that they need me to find their own sanctity. In no way is that true; and I think in no way is it also true that Jesus taught dependence on him for a sense of sanctity. He said to look inward and find the **child of humanity** within, unscathed with real sin. It is, in fact, my thinking that I am not complete and need another for that ideal that I "create sin" for myself. It is my thinking that I need to mingle with you to know my own sanctity that I sin. **Nothing in me is sinful, however. It is only in the way I deal with a sinless life that I "create sin" for myself.**

CHRIST – NOT A LAWMAN!

Many of the Christians who survived Christ offered themselves within a framework of law – just what Jesus rejected and asked those who could hear his message to reject. **Peter went about making law and became just another law giver by initiating the process of dogma, denying completely the soul of Jesus in terms of his request that we attend to the *child of humanity* within us as the only rule of life. No one needs any law – or dogma - to rule his or her life if they attend to the ideal of loving humanity.** How could there possibly be any other require-ment of true virtue? Loving humanity covers it all and does not allow exceptions. If you love humanity, there are no exceptions – including so called justice and judgment.

That the world is filled with law, offered to guide us to Heaven, is a clear indication to me that Jesus was not un-derstood as the proponent of self respect and other respect he was – and is. If I need ten ways to prove I love you, then clearly I have missed the boat in terms of knowing only one rule. **Dogma is nothing more than stating a whole bunch of thou shalts and thou shalt nots in or-der to keep me within some rule of order. Jesus tried to teach us that we should throw out all the dogma of the past and live only according to one rule – the rule of living life respecting the *child of humanity* or hu-manity as child within us and others.**

What have we done? We have not only retained all the old dogma, preserved from the **Old Law,** idealized by the **Ten Commandments**; but we have added volumes of new law in addition. Dogma was the way of life for the Jews when Jesus entered into their world; and dogma was the way of life for them when he left them. He came. They listened, but did not hear – anymore than we hear today.

As Jesus offers in **The Gospel of Thomas,** Verse 28, *empty we have come into this life and empty we seek to go out.* That is to say that we incarnate with a sense of individual meaninglessness and we die without a sense of individual meaning and sanctity. **Empty we come in – and empty we go out**. At least, that seems to be the case with many. And a huge part of our empty is seeing Jesus as a requirement of salvation, as a savior, when he told us to attend only to the *child of humanity* within us as the only rule of salvation. Like he offered elsewhere, just calling on Jesus does not save us. The only thing that saves us is knowing and living like we are holy unto ourselves because we are complete unto ourselves – being divine (Divine) expressions. All else is a form of empty.

THE DANGER OF LAW

Returning to the notion of not allowing ourselves to be subject to law, the consequences of obeying law, regardless of its source may well impact us past death. None of us know about that for sure, but I suspect that since souls are really the ones who make religious laws, if we live obliged to their law in life, we may have to submit to their control after life too. That should scare us into living outside of religious law as much as possible.

Why would I have to submit to religious law after death? Because I might be unaware that I actually died and may not know that the law of corporate life may not still apply. I do not know that such is so; but I can certainly imagine the possibility; and the possibility is quite enough for me to make sure I do not allow myself to be controlled by law in life – religiously.

It may well be in death what it was in life. In life, we circle ourselves with minds that agree with our values. In death, we may retain companionship with such minds. That may well be part of the justice of death. If I am greeted after I die, more than likely it will be by souls who divested themselves of law – or the need of it. That is, if that is the way I lived and the way I died. And if I lived thinking I need law to be complete, then most likely, if I am met by any souls or community of souls after I die, it will be by those who also feel a need for law. Even in death, those who live by need for law in life may still need law after death and be encompassed only by those with a similar need. I suspect that is the way it is, but I do not know for sure. No one does.

If such a notion of having to continue a state of mind after death is correct, however, only those who actually agree with Christ in reality will commune with him afterwards. That is to say nothing more than to live with me in the afterlife is to require that you are of the same mind as me – or Christ or anyone you might want to name. In truth, it may well be that to live with any desired soul – or be a companion thereof – I will have to be like that soul in order to be attracted by him or her or it. **By our selection of conduct and mindset, we may well be selecting our friends of a next experience. I expect that to be so.**

KINGDOM OF HEAVEN – MANY HOUSES INCLUDING *THE KINGDOM OF JESUS*

Like Jesus was reported to have said elsewhere, however, it is good to know that what we might think of as Heaven is likely comprised of many houses or mansions. One house may contain some who do not need law for completion. Another house may contain some who do; and there may be many rooms of varying mindsets within any given house. Though Jesus may not actually show up in a given law bound abode, those living there may still anticipate such a visit. It is like that in life. It may be like that in death. I guess that is to say, even bound by law after death may not be any worse than being bound by law before death.

And what a beautiful notion justice is. All of those who think they are getting away with crime in life may find themselves communing with fellow criminals in the hereafter; and those who shared a sense of compassion in life may well find themselves communing with like minded compassionate. The house or mansion or **Kingdom of Jesus** is only one of many possible experiences any of us can choose; but it's all Heaven – even if it's Hell because in it and through it, God is.

As Jesus says in **The Gospel of Thomas,** Verse 113, the *Kingdom of the Father is spread upon the earth and men do not see it.* "Father" here probably means "The God of All." Jesus may have added: **The Kingdom of the Father is spread about in the afterlife too and many do not see it there either.**

That which is considered the Kingdom of Jesus is often considered to be the same as the Kingdom of God or the Kingdom of the Father. You have to treat a word within its context, of course, and sometimes Jesus may have offered the Father as God and other times as a Kingdom he represents. In my mind, I see the Kingdom of Heaven or the Kingdom of the Father as used in Verse 113 of **The Gospel of Thomas** to merely represent **everywhere. The Kingdom of the Father is wherever God is. Since God is everywhere, then so also is Heaven or the Kingdom of the Father.**

Within the Kingdom of the Father or Heaven, however, there are many homes, so to speak. One of those homes could be called the **Kingdom of Jesus.** Everyone belongs to the Kingdom of the Father, given understood as Heaven, because everyone is where God is. Everyone does not belong to the **Kingdom of Jesus**, however. To belong to that, you have to be like Jesus and, in essence, live the ideal of loving the *child of humanity*.

I think that in the first verse of **The Gospel of Mary,** Jesus is really only defining his own ideal and asking us to consider it. That ideal is to see humanity as wholesome unto itself because it is of God. Others are free to choose the ideal they want, but Jesus is recommending his ideal as the best of possibilities. He offers that the way of law in terms of having to obey some edict outside of just respecting the *child of humanity* within us (**or our humanity as a child of God**) is to set ourselves up to being bound by the law and lawyers we accept.

Personally, I think that so many experiences that members of humanity have that offer some direction from what is considered **God** are nothing more than directions from some **community of saints** or souls who are bonded by some measure or other. I use the term "**saint**" loosely as descriptive of "**any soul who thinks they are doing what they should.**" Most of us are probably **saints** of our various communities. I suspect that souls who are outside of incarnation or fleshly housing have some ability to relate to those within bodies. We may know them as **angels** or **devils.** There may be a great deal of power related to any given community of saints or souls; and it could be such power that is often interpreted as **coming from God – or Satan -** when in actuality, it is only from some community of souls or some soul of bodiless status.

We should consider ourselves free to attend whatever ideal we choose, but if the ideal we choose is one of law, then quite likely we will bind ourselves within that community attending the law we choose – and it may not stop with death of body. By our choice of morals and companionship and companions, we may choose the ideal we want – and by it, our companions of the future as well. I suspect it is that way, though I do not know it for sure.

JESUS – ONLY AN ANGEL FOR HIS OWN *COMMUNITY OF SAINTS*

Jesus probably represented an **angel** from his own community of souls who think of God as merely the **Blessed of All**. Many do not act in life like we are all of God because of thinking that God is something that we must earn. Jesus knew that God is not something to be earned; but rather something infinite that is present in all. No one has to earn that which is already in them. His is a community of souls which are probably the most free of all souls in not having to abide by any law imposed from without. I believe that Jesus lived to try to free souls captive by law by encouraging them to live their lives free of law and bound only by the simple rule of respect for the ***child of humanity*** within us.

Most Christian churches do not agree, however. They see Jesus as being an extension of the **Laws of the Old Testament** and the completion of those laws. In my opinion, nothing could be further from the truth. **Jesus did not come to complete any law or set of laws related to attaining God or pleasing God. He came to challenge the laws that were – not confirm their authority.** And the reason? Because of the less than ideal quality of being bound within a structure of law.

Laws bind. *Rules guide.* At least within the context of this discussion, a law is a regulation or directive for which violation is punishable by an outside of self entity. A rule is a directive for which violation is not punishable by an outside of self entity. Violating a rule only concludes in the violator not reaching some worthy goal. Violating a law concludes – or can conclude – in some punishment of a violator. **The Kingdom of Jesus** is not about laws and no one will be punished for failure to comply with a Jesus directive. **The Kingdom of Jesus** is only about one rule – according to **The Gospel of Mary -** and that rule is to live life respecting the *child of humanity* or **our human nature** because it is of God. To violate the rule is not to be subject to punishment by Jesus for doing so. To violate the rule is simply to not qualify for **The Kingdom of Jesus**.

Unfortunately, many Christians know Jesus as a **Lawyer** or **Judge**, rather than as a **Ruler** – in terms of one who offers guidance. But as we know him, as lawyer or ruler, we will be claimed by a respective **communion of saints**. I see Peter as a lawyer – or judge or one given to law and wanting to bind by law and punish those who fail to obey his law. I see Jesus as a ruler – or one with a rule for himself that he wants to share with others – a rule that liberates a soul from being bound by some form of captive law. **Peter can condemn because failure to obey a law can be met with some arbitrary punishment. Jesus cannot condemn because failure to obey his rule only concludes with failure to know a life of virtue.**

PETER – LIKELY MISUNDERSTOOD JESUS

It is somewhat curious that people who condemn often blame that which is thought of as **The Holy Spirit** for their acts. As an example of that, in the fifth chapter of **Acts Of The Apostles** of the *BIBLE*, Peter condemns a couple who had just joined the new church for only giving half of their property to the new church. It was his judgment that this couple – Ananias and Sapphira – or a close spelling thereof – should give all their property, not just half of it. When he found out they had held back half of their donation, he called them to him and spit Hell and Damnation at them, but offered that it was **The Holy Spirit** who was really condemning them, not him, Peter. Peter literally scared them to death as each of them, one after the other, fell dead at his feet. Peter claimed it was **The Holy Spirit** who claimed them in death for *lying against The Holy Spirit*. We need go no further in the annals of Christianity beyond this story to know that it was not the Spirit of Jesus that Peter was following. **Jesus would have been thankful for any gift. Peter expressed anger that Ananias & Sapphira gave less that he demanded they give - and then damned them for not doing as he demanded.**

I get the sense from **The Gospel of Mary** that Peter had a hard time trying to understand Jesus; and because he had a hard time trying to understand him, in all likelihood, he never did. The story of Ananias and Sapphira in the fifth chapter of **Acts** proves that. In his ignorance, however, Peter may have assumed that no one could understand Jesus. Thus, one's misunderstanding of him is no worse than another's misunderstanding of him. He probably had no idea that others may have understood Jesus because he couldn't go there. In spite of having no real grasp of Jesus, however, he proceeded like he had known him and perhaps hoped that in some mystical Heaven, real understanding would come.

I suspect that is not the way it works, however. Real understanding probably does not come in the future if it is not experienced now. Sadly, Peter probably took his misunderstanding of Jesus and used an assumed love of Jesus as authority to create a church in the name of Jesus. Near as I can tell, that is most likely what happened. **The church as we have it today as one with a great love of law and willingness to punish or threaten punishment for disobedience is not what Jesus was about.** At least, I do not believe so.

It is a bit sad, but it is also just. It's sad because souls are not being liberated from living bound by law as Jesus wanted. It is just because many who think that they will see Jesus in Heaven but who live according to law probably will not see him – or be with him. They will be with their own kind, but not with Jesus. Regarding the issue of being able to join what might be called **The Kingdom of Jesus**, in the end, it won't matter if one of us claims he is Christian or not. It will only matter that we will have found liberation of soul by attending to the rule of loving the ***child of humanity***

within us – and within everyone. Notice in that expression the emphasis on the individual. Jesus says, look for the one child in you, not in the family of man.

THE INDIVIDUAL – THE ONLY PROPER FOCUS FOR A TRUE CHRISTIANITY

Between you and me, I suspect that which derailed a true Christianity was the idea that it was inherited through Judaism. Judaism put a tremendous emphasis on holiness through racial membership and family membership. The individual was lost in Judaism, near as I can tell. Just look at **The Ten Commandments.** Every emphasis in all those laws deals with one associated with another. In those commandments, the individual does not exist – from being bid to honor thy father and mother to not stealing another's wife. **It is this accent on meaning by relationship with others that I think Jesus tried so hard to dispel; and what most of the early fathers of the church tried so hard to maintain.**

People ask me, do you mean that you do not believe in **The Ten Commandments?** My answer to that is they are not needed for one who sees him or herself as independently holy. I have no interest in dishonoring my parents, but neither is it a concern. They have their life; and I have mine. Respect is sufficient; and respect is automatic if I know my worth because my worth is their worth. I have no interest in stealing another's wife because I have no need of any wife. Why would I want to steal a wife of another if I don't need any wife? I do not need a wife to complete me in my holiness because it is the Presence of God in me and in one who might be my wife that makes me holy. I certainly do not need a wife to attain holiness. So, you see, by accenting the holiness of the individual, at least many of the so called **Ten Commandments** are *obeyed* without any attention in doing so – and without the terrible control of law.

This is what Jesus tried to teach, I think; but because independent holiness would not serve the agents of power for releasing all souls from power, Jesus had to be squelched. Jesus was a Jew by heritage, it seems; and so, it almost naturally followed that in choosing Judaism as a birth place, he was sanctifying Judaism. That became the argument in order for those in power to retain it. In my opinion, as if you did not already know it, Jesus placed **NO importance on race or family** because his was an emphasis on individual holiness, totally independent of racial, national, or family ties.

Unfortunately, some erratic Jews offered Jesus to the world. I do not think they understood him in his plea for individual holiness and integrity. They had been racially, nationally, and family oriented and rather than allow Jesus to stand for the individual, they merely continued the Jewish customs of racial, national, and family importance. From that, we continue with all the insane ideas about man having to subject him or herself to the

greater good. Thus, Christ becomes a head of a family in Christ, just one step away from head of a Jewish race – or nation. Now you have everything slanted away from the individual and individual worth and right back to the nonsense that Jesus tried to dispel – that holiness is dependent upon a social context.

Dear, Dear Paul was very sincere, I think, in thinking he had it right in trying to emphasize the family – as would a good Jew. He could not let go of his Jewish doctrine, elevating family and race over the individual. He thought he was being very respectful of Jesus by claiming that Jesus was the head of a family in Christ. It sounds good; but it is not the basic message of Jesus. At least, I don't think it is.

It is, in fact, a derailment of true Christianity because individuals cannot stand on their own for their sanctity. They must depend on the head of the family – Jesus. With that dependence goes any sense of individual worth. Instead of souls going forward looking for the *child of humanity* within them as Jesus bid us to do via Mary Magdalene, we are set to look for the family of Christ and to be a member of the family of Christ. No one can go forward and claim sanctity outside of being a member of the family of Christ.

SOCIAL CHRISTIANITY – NOT ALL BAD

It is not all bad, of course. There is some good in thinking that way. Perhaps by sensing a family relationship with

Jesus as head, his doctrine of compassion does filter down in some. In others, however, who have no real compassion but think they are of the family of Christ, these are lost to their own whims and to the whims of their respective **community of saints**. For those communities – or families of souls – well, I guess they hold on to their own; and maybe that is the way it should be.

I think it good to keep in mind that membership in the **Kingdom of Jesus** is an option, not a requirement. No one has to belong; and, in deed, many are probably not well suited to belong;

but
what a wonderful world
it would be
if we were all members of a
True Kingdom of Jesus!
Would you not agree?

JESUS VIA MARY COMMENTARIES

§

THE END

The Key For Finding Peace

(Recitation with Refrain)
By
Francis William Bessler
Laramie, Wyoming
5/5/2005

REFRAIN:
What is the key for finding peace –
if you're human like me?
Well, Jesus told us long ago –
if peace we should like to know,
we can find it if we seek
within us – the child of humanity.

A long time ago, Jesus said –
please receive my peace,
but don't be led astray by those who know it not.
If someone says it's here or there –
or beyond where you can see,
do not be fooled.
I'll tell you how it should be sought.
Refrain.

Then Jesus said, listen to me –
I'll share with you my ways.
It is not near as hard as you may think it is.
You cannot find peace
by looking in that which rusts or decays.
Look within your image –
to find that which has no sin.
Refrain.

Jesus then continued to tell –
look for the child of humanity,
but do not look for it only in someone else.
The child of humanity is within you
and can make you free
if you'll just look at it –
and find an image of yourself.
Refrain.

Then Jesus said, listen here –
I'll tell you of my good news,
but the idea doesn't just belong to me.
For anyone who is human,
humanity itself is the truth;
for everything is from God –
in yourself, find Divinity.
Refrain.

So, let us, one and all –
preach the good news of the kingdom,
realizing it has always been within our reach.
The good news of the kingdom
is that we are equally human.
If peace is what we want –
only that can we teach.
Refrain (multiple times if desired).

Was Jesus a Messiah?

A Poem -
(though I have sung it free style too)
By
Francis William Bessler
Laramie, Wyoming
5/17/2006; modified slightly; 6/22/2015

Note:
The verses of this song have been derived
from verses found in my favorite gospels:
THE GOSPELS OF
THOMAS and MARY MAGDALENE

Was Jesus a messiah –
or was he just like you and me?
Did we give him all his power –
to avoid being free?
Is Heaven another place –
or is it just knowing God inside?
Is Hell only insisting –
on refusing to be kind?

Was Jesus a messiah –
or was he just like you and me?
Have we turned away from the truth –
of our mutual Divinity?
Did Jesus really tell us –
that the Kingdom is within?
Did he really say –
there is no such thing as sin?

Was Jesus a messiah –
or was he just like you and me?
Have we known Jesus all along –
or have we been deceived?
Did Jesus really tell us –
that we should all be as a child?
Does that only mean –
we should be equal all the while?

Was Jesus a messiah –
or was he just like you and me?
Did he really tell us –
to find our child of humanity?
Is life nothing more –
than endless mystery?
Is worth only knowing –
all are of the same Divinity?

Was Jesus a messiah –
or was he just like you and me?
Was he only more aware –
of what allows us to be free?
Is it really true –
that to be a part of his family,
al I have to do –
is live my life shamelessly?

Was Jesus a messiah –
or was he just like you and me?
Did he only realize –
God is in all equally?
Did he really say –
we should take off our clothes
because we should have no shame –
for the life God's bestowed?

Is Jesus a messiah –
or is he just like you and me?
Is he smiling now –
because the truth is finally free?
Is virtue only knowing –
that we are all the same –
and that we need no messiah –
when we live without shame?

Peace On Earth

By
Francis William Bessler
Laramie, Wyoming
7/31/2007;4th verse added 9/26/2015

REFRAIN:
There can be Peace on Earth –
for all the world to see.
There can be Peace on Earth –
but it must begin with me.
There'll be Peace on Earth –
when we all see Divinity.
But there can be no peace –
without me.

What is peace, my friends?
It's knowing that you belong;
and it's knowing that we're all the same.
That is peace, my friends
as we're singing in this song;
and it's not holding anyone to blame.
Refrain.

What is peace, my friends?
It's loving what we are;
and it's knowing that all life is a gift.
That is peace, my friends
and if we're ever to stop war,
we must believe that all life is blessed.
Refrain.

What is peace, my friends?
It's failure to hold a grudge;
and it's forgiving to be forgiven.
That is peace, my friends
and it's the only way to judge
our way into that lovely state of Heaven.
Refrain.

What is peace, my friends?
It's knowing all Creation is right;
and it's knowing everything is good.
That is peace, my friends
and if we're ever to live in the light,
we must realize all's one big Brotherhood.
Refrain (several times).

Hello, Everybody!

A song by
Francis William Bessler
12/3/2011

REFRAIN:
Hello, Everybody, it's time to smile.
Hello, Everybody, your time's worth while.
Hello, Everybody, know you are a mystery.
Whether you're a boy or a girl,
you're a son of Divinity.

When I look out a window
to see a tree leafed in green,
I become aware
of a greater truth that is unseen.
All that's in that lovely tree
is also found in me.
The tree & I are one
as we both share eternity.
Refrain.

When I look up into the sky,
I see a Sun shining bright;
and I become aware
that all's dependent upon the light.
All that's found upon
our wonderful, plentiful Earth
depends on the light of the Sun
for its very birth.
Refrain.

When I look out into space,
I'm sure no end can be;
and I realize that all must be
lost within Infinity.
No one can know where it ends -
anymore than where it begins.
Just be happy you're part of it all -
and to that, just say, Amen.
Refrain.

When I look into the future,
I see that same ole tree
that is in my present now
and shares my mystery;
and I know the tree & I
will go forward as we've done,
knowing that we are among
Life's blessed sons.
Refrain (2).

Ending:
Yes, whether you're a boy or a girl,
you're a son of Divinity.
Whether you're a boy or a girl,
you're a son of Divinity.

The Same

By
Francis William Bessler
Laramie, Wyoming
9/15/2008

REFRAIN:
I'm the same – as everyone.
I'm the same – and I'm having fun.
I'm the same as you, my friend;
and I'll be the same – beyond the end.

(The following could be added –
or featured only at end of song.)

You're the same – as everyone.
You're the same – you should be having fun.
You're the same as me, my friend;
and you'll be the same – beyond the end.

The rule of life is that you will be
just what you allow within your dreams.
Tomorrow will be like today
in the manner of soulful ways.

If you're kind today, it will be the same
when tomorrow comes, be it night or day;
and if you're cruel now, you'll continue on
just as you are when tomorrow comes.
Refrain
(though it may be skipped too).

People think they need to be different
in order to make life of consequence;
but no matter how much they insist it's so,
underneath, they're the same in Nature's clothes.
If you think you can change the way things are
by finding strength in various wars,
you're only pretending some life's not good
and blowing a chance for true brotherhood.
Refrain
(though it may be skipped too).

In the Gospel of Thomas, Jesus said to Salome,
when he was asked of whom he was a son,
he said, I am one who is from the Same
Light as me, thus having no shame.
And it's just like that with each of us
from whom we come should be our trust.
Well, we come from Nature and the Divine

and that is what should be our pride.
Refrain
(though it may be skipped too).

Many people are afraid to die
because they think Nature's a lie.
They think that death should never be
but that is not the way it seems to me.
I look at life and it seems clear
that all things die – so I should have no fear
of anything beyond because the truth
must be the same for me as it is for you.
Refrain
(though it may be skipped too).

What will happen when I die?
Probably more of the same as in life.
There is no reason for me to believe
that my soul will change radically.
As I was before, I will become again,
I will see me as virtuous or filled with sin.
If my soul continues – and the notion's sane,
it will continue on and be the same.
Refrain
(though it may be skipped too).

So, let us all join and celebrate
the wonder of our common state.
We are the same in what's there to find.
Our bodies are alike – as too our minds.
What you really are, I am too –
and that, my friend, is a basic truth.
The way I treat you becomes my refrain
simply because we are the same.
Refrain
(multiple times if wished).

ABOUT THE AUTHOR

§

FRANCIS WILLIAM BESSLER WAS BORN on December 3, 1941, the seventh of Leo and Clara Bessler's eight children. He was raised Roman Catholic on a small farm outside Powell, Wyoming.

Bessler spent six years studying for the Catholic ministry, beginning with Latin studies at St. Lawrence Seminary in Mount Calvary, Wisconsin, in 1960. He then entered St. Thomas Seminary in Denver, Colorado in the fall of 1961.

Bessler loved his seminary years, but in the spring of 1966, the Rector of St. Thomas, one Father Danagher, told the young man his thinking "was not that of a Catholic priest." Bessler's dogma professor went further, labeling him a heretic for insisting faith must be subject to understanding—a belief Bessler maintains to this day.

More information about Bessler and his life is available at www.una-bella-vita.com. Father Danagher was right, but that doesn't mean Bessler's insistence that faith requires understanding is wrong.

§

*(Main Theme: **Life Is Divine, Sinless, Sacred, & Worthy**)*

Available from Amazon.com and other retailers.
Also, see website www.una-bella-vita.com.

To order online via Amazon.com,
or other retailers,
enter "Francis Bessler"
in the search bar of Amazon.com.
or any other book store.

Prices vary from $14 to $28 -
depending upon size of book.

All books also available via Kindle

1.
WILD FLOWERS
(about 270 pages)
(essays and songs

mostly written as website blogs
from 2012 to 2014)
Printed in a smaller font 2 type.

2.

FIVE HEAVEN ON EARTH STORIES
(about 420 pages)
(Featuring 5 philosophical stories
written from 1975 - 2007)
Printed in a larger font 4 type
for the benefit of an easier read.

3.

EXPLORING THE SOUL -
And BROTHER JESUS
(about 200 pages)
(Featuring an analysis of several theories
about the origin and destiny of the soul -
and supplying an original idea too -
originally written in 1988.
Also, featuring a new look at Jesus
via an essay series written in 2005)
Printed in a larger font 4 type
for the benefit of an easier read.

4.

JOYFUL HAPPY SOUNDS!
(about 470 pages)

(featuring all of my songs and poems
written from 1963 to 2015; total: 198)
Printed in a smaller font 2 type.

5.

LOVING EVERYTHING
(WILD FLOWERS # 2)
(about 350 pages)
(essays and songs mostly written
as website blogs from 2014 to 2015,
though songs often predate 2014 too)
Printed in a smaller font 2 type.

6.

JESUS
ACCORDING TO
THOMAS & MARY -
AND ME
(about 260 pages)
(Featuring The Gospels of Thomas & Mary
and a personal interpretation of each)
Printed in a larger font 4 type
for the benefit of an easier read.

7.

IT'S A NEW DAY!
(WILD FLOWERS # 3)
(about 470 pages)

(essays and songs mostly written
as website blogs from 2016 to 2017,
though items often predate 2016 too -
and 5 new songs since 2015
have been added as well).
Printed in a larger font 4 type
for benefit of an easier read.

8.

IMPRESSIONS OF FRANCIS & WILLIAM
(about 140 pages)
(featuring essay works written in 1994
about two of history:
St. Francis of Assisi (1182-1226)
&
William Penn (1644-1718).
Printed in a larger font 4 type
for the benefit of an easier read.

Jesus - According To Thomas & Mary - and Me

§

The End

Made in the USA
Columbia, SC
31 January 2018